AN INTRODUCTION TO
METAPHYSICS

AN INTRODUCTION TO
METAPHYSICS

C. H. WHITELEY
formerly Professor of Philosophy
University of Birmingham

THE HARVESTER PRESS · SUSSEX
HUMANITIES PRESS · NEW JERSEY

This edition first published in 1977 by
THE HARVESTER PRESS LIMITED
Publisher: John Spiers
2 Stanford Terrace, Hassocks, Sussex
and in the USA in 1977 by
Humanities Press Inc.,
Atlantic Highlands, New Jersey 07716

First published 1950 by
Methuen & Co. Ltd., London
Reprinted 1955, 1964, 1966.

British Library Cataloguing in Publication Data

Whiteley, Charles Henry
    An Introduction to metaphysics. – [1st ed. reprinted]
    1.   Metaphysics
    I.   Title
    110   BD111
    ISBN 0–85527–126–4

Library of Congress Cataloging in Publication Data

Whiteley, Charles Henry.
    An introduction to metaphysics.
    Includes index.
    1.   Metaphysics.   I.   Title.
BD131.W56   1977   110   77–1892

ISBN 0–391–00711–4

Printed in Great Britain by
REDWOOD BURN LIMITED
Trowbridge & Esher

PREFACE TO FIRST EDITION

This book is intended mainly for those without much experience in philosophy. Such a book should, in my opinion, deal principally with problems which seem to the general reader worthy of serious study, rather than with those more technical questions in logic and theory of knowledge which are apt to appear trivial until one understands their implications. It should also, as far as possible present connected arguments and definite points of view, and avoid breaking up into disconnected fragments discussions which properly belong together. The scarcity of good introductory books on philosophy which satisfy these requirements is my reason for attempting to satisfy them myself in this book.

I am grateful to Prof. L. J. Russell, who has remedied some weaknesses in the subject-matter, and to my wife, who has corrected the worst defects of the style.

C. H. WHITELEY

PREFACE TO 1977 EDITION

Since this book was written a great deal of progress has been made in discovering physico-chemical explanations of biological processes, and in accounting for human behaviour by reference to physical states of the human body. The materialist assumption that everything that happens is ultimately explicable in terms of the laws of physics is year by year more strongly confirmed

The Phenomenalist view, which in 1949 was popular enough to deserve a good deal of attention, has since fallen into disrepute.

In the philosophy of mind, it is now generally held that when we talk of "the mind" and of its states and activities – desires, emotions, love and hate, knowing and understanding – we are not referring merely to private states of consciousness; a reference to specific kinds of publicly observable behaviour and tendencies to behave is involved in the meanings of these words, and unless this was so we could not know the truth of the statements we make about the minds of others. I think this is correct, and must admit that in places in this book where I wrote of "mind" as though it was equivalent to "consciousness", I have written misleadingly. But I remain convinced that we are able to think and talk about states of consciousness apart from their bodily manifestations, and that the relation between consciousness and physical processes is the crucial problem in this area.

Much has been written recently in support of one solution to this problem which in 1949 I dismissed rather brusquely – namely, that states of consciousness are identical with states of the brain. This view so simplifies our interpretation of the universe and fits so neatly into the scientific picture that it needs to be taken seriously. But I cannot convince myself that the description of my brain as a congeries of particles and movements distinguished only by elementary physical properties can also be a description of my unitary conscious experience with its immense variety of qualities of sensation and feeling.

I have given my views on these questions in the philosophy of mind in "Mind in Action" (Oxford University Press 1973).

C. H. WHITELEY

CONTENTS

GLOSSARY

Some of the words here given are terms peculiar to philosophy. But many of them are words in common use, which philosophers use in special senses different from, or more precise than, their ordinary senses. For this reason it is worth while for beginners to look through this Glossary before starting to read philosophical literature.

A POSTERIORI, A PRIORI. An *a posteriori* idea is an idea derived from something which the thinker has observed ; an *a posteriori* belief is one arrived at on the evidence of observation. An *a priori* idea is one not derived from observation ; an *a priori* belief is one arrived at independently of observation.

ABSOLUTE, see Relative.

ABSTRACT, ABSTRACTION. Abstraction is the consideration of some quality or relation of things without regard to the other qualities and relations with which it is associated. Thinking is abstract in so far as it considers some features of a situation and ignores others.

ACCIDENT, see Essence.

AESTHETICS. The theory of beauty.

BEHAVIOURISM. A psychological method in which human beings are regarded as material objects behaving in certain characteristic ways, and no attention is paid to their " consciousness " in explaining this behaviour.

CATEGORY. A very general characteristic, or way of being. A list of categories attempts to include all the types of qualities and relations anything may possess.

COGNITION, COGNITIVE. A general term for all experiences of knowing, believing, thinking, supposing, wondering, observing, etc.

DEDUCTION, INDUCTION. A deductive argument is one in which the conclusion follows necessarily, i.e., with certainty, from the premises ; e.g., an argument in which an instance of a general principle is inferred from that general principle. An inductive argument is one in which a general principle is inferred from particular instances.

DEFINITION. A definition of X is a description which applies to X and does not apply to anything except X.

DEISM. See Theism.

DETERMINISM. The doctrine that everything that happens is in all respects determined by preceding events, and could have been different only if the preceding events had been different.

DISCURSIVE. See Intuition.

DUALISM. See Monism.

EMPIRICAL, EMPIRICISM. An empirical belief is one based on experience ;
as empiric, one who relies on experience rather than theory.
Empiricism is the doctrine that all our knowledge is derived from
experience.

EPIPHENOMENALISM. The doctrine that all mental events are entirely
determined by physical events, and do not themselves determine
anything.

EPISTEMOLOGY. The theory of knowledge, including the theory of belief
and other kinds of thinking.

ESSENCE, ESSENTIAL. The essential attributes of a thing, constituting its
essence, are those attributes which it must have in order to be the
thing it is ; other attributes are called " accidents."

ETHICS. The theory of right and wrong conduct.

FINAL CAUSE. The final " cause " (reason or explanation) of a thing is
the purpose it is intended to serve.

HEDONISM. Psychological hedonism is the doctrine that the attainment
of pleasure (and the avoidance of pain) is the aim of all human action.
Ethical hedonism is the doctrine that the attainment of pleasure (and
the avoidance of pain) ought to be the aim of all human action.

HEURISTIC. A heuristic assumption is an assumption made, not because
there are adequate reasons for believing it to be true, but because by
assuming it we can discover other truths.

HYPOTHESIS. A proposition put forward, not as something which is true,
but as something which may be true, to be tested by working out its
consequences and comparing them with the observed facts.

IDEA. This word has many different uses in different types of philosophy.
  (1) It has its ordinary non-philosophical sense in which " to have an
      idea of X " means to think about X or to have some beliefs
      about X. Philosophers often use " concept " in this sense.
  (2) In Descartes, Locke, etc., the term is widened to include not only
      thoughts, but also sensations and all kinds of mental imagery :
      Locke says he means by " idea " " whatever is the object of
      understanding when a man thinks."
  (3) Berkeley in his best-known works uses " idea " to mean an im-
      pression of sensation (sense-datum) or of imagination, memory,
      or dream, and this only.
  (4) The original sense of the term in philosophy, but not the
      commonest, is that of Plato : his " ideas " or " forms " are types
      or standards to which observable things more or less closely
      conform. Plato thought that these Ideas existed of themselves
      apart from our thought, but later philosophers have held that
      they exist only in thought.

IDEALISM. In ordinary speech an Idealist is (*a*) one who has high and
difficult ideals, and (*b*) (disparagingly) one who pursues unattainable
ideals, or confuses the ideal with the actual. In philosophy Idealism
is the doctrine that reality consists entirely of minds or spirits and
their experiences (" ideas.")

IMMANENT. See Transcendent.

INDUCTION. See Deduction.

INTROSPECTION. A person's awareness of himself and his own mental processes while they are actually going on.

INTUITION, INTUITIVE. We have intuitive knowledge of a fact when we know it by direct apprehension, and not by inference from our knowledge of something else ; inferential knowledge is sometimes called " discursive."

MATERIALISM. In philosophy, the doctrine that everything that exists consists of Matter.

MECHANISM. A mechanistic explanation is one which explains the nature of a whole as entirely derived from the nature of its parts. In biology, Mechanism is the view that the behaviour of living organisms can be explained by a knowledge of the chemical and physical properties of their parts, as opposed to Vitalism, which holds that one must suppose some special " vital principle " in addition.

METAPHYSICS. The theory of the nature of the universe as a whole, and of those general principles which are true of everything that exists.

MONISM. Opposed to Dualism, Monism holds that there is only one kind of substance in the universe, Dualism that there are two, the material and the mental. Opposed to Pluralism, Monism holds that all things are parts of one all-inclusive substance, Pluralism that there are many independent substances.

NOMINALISM. See Realism.

NORMATIVE. Laying down standards of what is right and wrong, or correct and incorrect.

OBJECT, OBJECTIVE, SUBJECT, SUBJECTIVE. Usually in philosophy Subject means the observer, thinker, or experiencer, and Object whatever he is aware of. Whatever in experience proceeds from the subject is called " subjective " ; whatever is independent of the subject and his awareness is called " objective."

ONTOLOGY. The theory of being and of the kinds of beings.

OPTIMISM. Technically, the theory that this is the best of all possible worlds.

PANTHEISM. See Theism.

PERCEPTION. See Sensation.

PHENOMENON. Whatever can be observed.

PHENOMENALISM. The doctrine that all statements about material objects can be analysed into statements about actual or possible sensations.

PHENOMENOLOGY. The systematic description of the various types of experience : the description of particular facts in such a way as to bring out their underlying principle.

PLURALISM. See Monism.

POSITIVISM   The view that the description of phenomena, and of the order of their occurrence, comprises the whole of human knowledge.

PRAGMATISM.   A pragmatic test of a theory is a test of how it works in practice.   Pragmatism is the theory that the whole meaning of any conception expresses itself in practical consequences ; a true belief is one which it is useful to hold.

PROPOSITION.   Whatever may be believed, disbelieved, known, doubted, asserted, denied, or supposed.

RATIONALISM.   Has two quite different senses.   (1) The view that no beliefs ought to be accepted by " faith " or on authority, but only those which " reason " finds ground for judging true.   (2) The doctrine that reason is a source of knowledge independent of sense-perception ; opposed to Empiricism.

REALISM.   Also has two quite distinct senses.   (1) Chiefly in mediæval philosophy, the doctrine that universals have a real existence independently of their instances ; opposed to Nominalism, which holds that there are no universals, but only common names.   (2) In modern philosophy, usually the doctrine that we can be aware of realities which exist independently of our awareness of them ; opposed to Idealism.

RELATIVE, RELATIVISM, RELATIVITY ; ABSOLUTE.   A property is relative when it belongs to a thing only because of that thing's relation to another thing ; it is absolute when it belongs to a thing whatever its relations to other things.   Thus " The Absolute " (the absolutely real) is that which is real independently of everything else.   The physical theory of relativity holds that certain measurements of time vary according to the rates of motion of the measuring instruments relatively to the things measured.   Ethical relativism holds that what is right and wrong varies according to the different characters, experiences and customs of different persons and societies.

SENSE, SENSATION, PERCEPTION.   In philosophy " sense " usually refers to " the five (or more) senses," and " sensible " usually means " perceptible through the senses " ; the words are rarely used as in " good sense " and " a sensible man."   There is no consistent distinction between Sensation and Perception, but many philosophers use Sensation to mean sense-experience apart from the interpretation put upon it, and Perception to mean the interpretation of that experience.   Thus I sense a rumbling noise, but perceive an approaching train.

SENSUM, SENSE-DATUM.   What one is directly aware of in sense-experience— colour-patches, sounds, etc.

SOLIPSISM.   The theory that nothing exists except me.

SUBJECT.   See Object.

SUBSTANCE.   Distinguished from qualities and relations as that which has qualities and stands in relations.   In older philosophy Substance is used in a more restricted senses, as that which is capable of existing by itself.   It is also sometimes equivalent to Essence.

SYNTHESIS. The putting together of items to make a whole ; opposed to Analysis.

TAUTOLOGY. A statement which one may know to be true merely by knowing the meanings of the terms employed in it.

TELEOLOGY. Purposiveness.

THEISM. In a general sense, any kind of belief in the existence of God. In a more special sense, Theism is the belief in a personal God distinct in nature from the world but active within it. It is contrasted with Deism, which holds that God's nature and activities are quite separate from that of anything in the world ; and with Pantheism, which holds that the world has no distinct existence apart from God.

TRANSCENDENT. To transcend is to go beyond. A transcendent God is one who exists apart from the rest of the universe ; an immanent God. one who is present in the world. " The transcendent " is very often that which transcends *experience*, i.e., cannot be experienced, or cannot be completely experienced.

UNIVERSAL. A quality or relation which can be common to many different things ; e.g., whiteness, justice. The instances of a universal are called " particulars."

UTILITARIANISM. In a general sense ; the theory that right conduct is that which produces the greatest good. In a more special sense, the theory that right conduct is that which produces the greatest happiness.

VITALISM. See Mechanism.

I

INTRODUCTION

I.—POPULAR PHILOSOPHY AND ACADEMIC PHILOSOPHY

AN INTRODUCTION to philosophy ought to begin by explaining what philosophy is. On this question, unfortunately, there are wide differences of opinion, especially between the professional philosopher and the intelligent man in the street. The latter, when he turns to philosophy, usually expects it to provide him with an enlightening and satisfying interpretation of the universe. He wants to be instructed as to " the meaning of life " and " the nature of ultimate reality." He wants a firm basis for his thinking and his scheme of living, a unified view of things which will make him feel at home in the world. Nothing could seem less likely to satisfy these needs than the sort of discussion which is to be heard at congresses of philosophers, or read in their professional journals. The present-day academic philosopher is inclined to concentrate his attention on technical problems in logic, such as " Are there any a priori synthetic propositions ? " " Do universals really exist ? " " Can the notion of cause be defined in terms of regular sequence ? " It may even appear as if his main concern is not to describe the nature of the world, but only to catalogue the meanings of various words and phrases in which other people describe it. In any case he has little to say which will help the ordinary man in the solution of his philosophical problems. So there seem to be at least two different notions of the nature of philosophy, that of the man in the street and that of the professional philosopher.

What is the reason for this difference ? It is not that the philosophers themselves are uninterested in the great and serious problems which the man in the street propounds. Most philosophers philosophise because they like to ; yet I doubt whether there is one of them who was first attracted to the subject through wanting an answer to the fiddling problems of verbal analysis which now occupy so much of his attention. The professional, like the amateur philosopher, begins by seeking answers to fundamental problems about the nature of the world. There are two reasons why his attention has been diverted from these to other problems which seem more trivial.

The first reason is that, unlikely as it may seem, the answers to the important questions do depend to a considerable extent on the solutions we find to the trivial ones. I hope to show later something of the way in which, in trying to decide what is the meaning of life or the nature of ultimate reality, we are inevitably brought to grips with other problems which seem to have little to do with these questions : how, in particular, certain issues in logic and theory of knowledge have an important bearing on our conclusions.

2.—UNANSWERABLE QUESTIONS

The second reason for the discrepancy between the popular and the academic views of philosophy requires more explanation. It is that the professional philosopher often finds that the questions put to him by the interested outsider are not answerable in a way which will give satisfaction to the questioner, and at the same time be firmly grounded on sound reasons.

Unanswerable questions are of many kinds. Some of them, like " What is the meaning of life ? ", " What is the nature of ultimate reality ? ", are very vague. So, in order to answer them, we have to spend much time and trouble in finding out what they can mean ; and by the time we have made them definite enough to be capable of an answer, the man in the street may hardly recognize them as his own questions. In asking them, he is often unsure what sort of an answer will really content him. He is not looking for a definite item to fill a definite gap in his picture of the world, as he might look for a missing piece in a jigsaw puzzle. He is trying to relieve a general, diffused sense of bewilderment. Thus a great part of the philosopher's business consists in the clarifying of problems, and in teaching us to ask the right questions, which in philosophy is often more than half way to finding the right answers.

Sometimes, again, the questions asked of the philosopher cannot be answered because they are not really *questions*. Thus, when a man asks " What is the meaning of life ? ", his motive may indeed be partly curiosity about the nature of the world, which can be satisfied by giving him correct information about things as they are. But it is likely that he is impelled by an additional motive, an uneasiness of the soul, a sense of emptiness or bewilderment in the face of things that must be done and endured. His difficulty is not in analysing, classifying, and connecting phenomena, but in appraising, valuing, and appreciating them. He is in search of something which he can approve, enjoy, pursue, or serve. Now no set of true statements about the nature of things will by themselves satisfy this need. A man may know all the facts there are to be known about the world, and still feel the lack of interest and purpose in life, the uncertainty of aim, which first made him ask philosophical questions. He needs, not a theory, but a cure. A nerve tonic, a love affair, the influence of a compelling personality, may provide it, but philosophical truth will not.

Finally, the philosopher may turn away from the discussion of fundamental problems about the nature of things because he simply does not know the answers, and entertains no hope of discovering them. He believes that, if they can be answered at all, it is not by the methods in which he is expert ; it is therefore a waste of time for him to discuss them. And so he prefers to concentrate upon those narrower and more manageable logical problems to which he sees some hope of a definite solution.

3.—PHILOSOPHY AND SCIENCE

This shrinkage of the philosopher's domain is a modern development. When the word " philosophy " began to be used by the Greeks about 500 years B.C., it meant " love of wisdom " ; that is, it did not denote a department of knowledge, but an interest or attitude of mind. What made a man a philosopher was the way he thought about things, rather than the particular things he thought about. In fact, the earliest Greek philosophers loved wisdom of almost every kind, and speculated freely on a great variety of topics : mathematics, physics, biology, jurisprudence, literary criticism, were all branches of " philosophy." Physics is still referred to as " natural philosophy " in some old-established universities.

The separation from philosophy of these other branches of knowledge has come about in the main since the seventeenth century ; and its chief cause has been the development of that technique of discovery which we now call " scientific." Scientific method comprises : (1) the careful and exact observation of phenomena of a particular type, and the precise measurement of all their measurable properties ; (2) the classification and comparison of these observed facts, to discover which phenomena are regularly associated with one another ; (3) the framing of general laws by which these regularities may be explained ; and (4) the testing of these laws by further observations, and especially by that observation under artificially controlled conditions which is called " experiment." The scientist's aim is the discovery of " laws of nature," that is, generalisations of the form, " Whenever A, then B " ; and, in the end, the only evidence he will accept for the validity of a law of nature is that things are observed to happen in conformity with it. The method by which a general law is inferred from observed instances of it is called " inductive."

For the past 300 years, scientific method has been successfully applied over an increasingly wide field, replacing the method of armchair speculation and discussion associated with philosophy. So, first the study of physical nature, and more recently the study of the mind and of human society, have passed out of the hands of the philosophers and into the hands of various groups of specialised scientific workers. There is now left to the modern philosopher only that part of the ancestral estate which cannot be cultivated by scientific methods. What fields of knowledge are there which do not belong to science ?

4.—LOGIC

The traditional answer to this question classifies philosophical, as distinct from scientific, problems under three heads. First, there is that thinking about thinking itself for which the general name is Logic. The subject-matter of Logic is the technique of reasoning. Its aim is not to examine, as the psychologist does, the ways in which people actually argue, but to distinguish good arguments from bad, to make clear what sorts of reasons are good reasons for holding beliefs of particular kinds. The difference between good and bad reasons is not the same as that between true and false opinions ; a man may argue illogically to a true conclusion, or logically to a false conclusion, if his premises are false or inadequate. So Logic does not tell us which of our beliefs are true. It enables us to make the most of the information we have, to think more clearly, consistently, and systematically. It helps us to distinguish between what can be proved, what must be taken for granted, and what can only be conjectured. And, since the principal tool of human thinking is language, logicians give much attention to the ways in which language is used, and the ways in which its use could be improved.

5.—ETHICS, AESTHETICS

A second type of philosophical problem is that concerned with right and wrong, good and bad, in human conduct and institutions, forming the subject-matter of Ethics or Moral Philosophy, and of Social and Political Philosophy ; with which we may group the problems of beauty and ugliness which are the subject-matter of Aesthetics. These too lie outside the field of science. From time to time, indeed, some thinker or other issues a demand for a " scientific " ethics or political philosophy or æsthetics, or, worse still, claims the honourable title of " scientific " for some view of his own on these topics. The demand cannot be satisfied, and the claim, whoever makes it, cannot be allowed. There are certainly plenty of scientific problems concerning human conduct and human valuations, and the solution of them should be sought in a scientific manner. But scientific investigation will tell us only how people in fact do behave under given conditions ; it cannot tell us how they *ought* to behave under those conditions. Laws of nature can have nothing to say about good and evil. There are no observable facts which will settle the question whether criminal lunàtics ought to be put to death, or whether Picasso's paintings are things of beauty. We may agree about all the *facts* of the case, and still dispute about the verdict. So, when the scientist has provided the facts, it is left to the philosopher to discuss the valuations.

To do this he must reflect, and make others reflect, upon their moral or æsthetic judgments, trying to discover what men really do find good and beautiful, what it is in a moral action or a work of art which induces them to approve or admire it. Such reflection can make men's appreciation of values keener and more refined, and their judgments more consistent. But the moral philosopher cannot prove his conclusions, as the scientist can, or produce any final settlement of those differences of moral judgment which arise. It is of the greatest importance to keep clear the difference between judgments of fact, which *can* be proved or disproved by the evidence of observation, and judgments of value, which cannot. Much confusion in thinking about human problems is caused by mixing up description with appraisal; when people talk about "rights," about "exploitation," about "genius," and so on, it is often very hard to discover whether what they are saying is matter for science or for philosophy.

6.—METAPHYSICS

Most systems of philosophy have something to say both about knowledge and about conduct. Nevertheless, when we talk of "a philosophy," it is usually neither a logical nor an ethical doctrine that we are thinking of. The central and principal part of philosophy is that which tries to deal, not with any part or aspect of reality, but with the whole, and to provide us with a comprehensive picture of what the universe is in its completeness. This third branch of philosophy, which is concerned with the general nature of reality, was called "first philosophy" by Aristotle, and is now generally known as Metaphysics. Under this head come discussions about the nature of Matter and of Mind and how they are related, of the existence and nature of God, of the freedom of the human will, of the immortality of the soul.

Now as to the proper place of metaphysics in the scheme of human knowledge, philosophers themselves dispute fiercely. Some of them regard metaphysics as the greatest, the most important, the most fundamental of all the varieties of human knowledge, the "queen of the sciences" whose laws all other branches of thought must obey. But there are others who deny that there is such a branch of knowledge at all, and use the word "metaphysical" as a term of abuse carrying the imputation of emptiness and sophistry. These philosophers do not, of course, mean that the problems called "metaphysical" are silly or unimportant. Their complaint is about the way these problems are handled by professed "metaphysicians." The dispute is a dispute about method.

7.—RATIONALISTS AND EMPIRICISTS

The defenders of metaphysics have usually maintained that the human mind has the capacity of knowing certain general truths about the nature of reality by a direct insight of the reason, apart from the detailed information given by the observations of the senses. Hence, they say, metaphysics can be carried on independently of science. By pure thought we can discover some first principles which are evident and certain ; they cannot be overthrown by any subsequent experience or scientific thinking, but on the contrary are presupposed by all such thinking. To think out and expound these first principles is the task of the metaphysician, and he is able to perform it by the exercise of his reason without assistance from the detailed findings of the scientists. This view is known as " rationalism."* On the other side, the " empiricists " or " positivists " maintain that the only way of learning the nature of the world is the method of the sciences, the inductive method of generalisation from " experience "—that is, from observed facts. Problems which cannot be solved by scientific methods cannot, according to the empiricists, be solved at all ; and metaphysics, which discusses such problems, is not a branch of knowledge, but a kind of parlour game, all the more entertaining because you are allowed to make your own rules, and elaborate the most charming theories with no risk of being caught out by awkward facts. The metaphysician may speculate as he pleases about the next world, which is beyond the reach of observation ; but it is the scientist who takes care of us in this one.

I shall make no attempt to discuss the validity of Rationalism and Empiricism as theories of knowledge ; that is a very complex subject. I shall say only that a method of inquiry must be justified by its results ; and, judged by its results, the rationalist method in metaphysics is a failure. It has had a full and fair trial. The efforts of many men of outstanding genius have been devoted to it. But the result has not been the building up of a solid body of metaphysical knowledge, carrying conviction to all reasonable men. It has been the construction of a great number of different

*The word " rationalism " has other meanings : see Glossary.

chemes by different philosophers, varying in almost every possible way, and getting no nearer to agreement on the main issues with the passage of the centuries. Men whose background of experience was similar have often found themselves in agreement ; but men belonging to different societies and periods, and of different casts of mind, have come to different conclusions. We are forced to admit that a proposition may seem self-evident to a highly intelligent philosopher, and still not be true. In the meantime the scientists, patiently following their method of observation, hypothesis, and experiment, have, step by step, constantly increased our stock of agreed and reliable truths about the world we live in.

In this book, therefore, I shall make the empiricist assumption that the only way to learn the truth about the world is to observe it, and to interpret those parts of it which we cannot observe, by analogy with those parts which we can observe. This method will give us no short cuts to ultimate truth, and no absolute certainties ; for the evidence of experience is always in principle liable to be contradicted by fresh experience. But it is the best that we can do. On this view there is no hard-and-fast line between scientific and metaphysical problems. But this does not mean that the various special sciences between them cover the whole of human knowledge and leave nothing at all for the philosopher to do. There are still questions which can reasonably be called metaphysical, and which do not fall within the compass of any scientific study.

8.—THE SCOPE OF METAPHYSICS

(1) There are plenty of important questions to which science has as yet given us no answer, either because its technique of exact measurement and experimental investigation cannot, in the present state of knowledge, be applied to them, or because the scientific evidence is too scanty or too ambiguous. Many questions relating to the more complex performances of the human mind, and to the relations between

the mind and the body, are in this condition. But, though on such matters there may be no accepted scientific truth, nevertheless there are more reasonable and less reasonable opinions about them. And it is worth while to discuss the possibilities as carefully and thoroughly as we can, so that we can disentangle the more reasonable views from the others, bring out more clearly the problems at issue, and get a step nearer towards working out ways of solving them scientifically. In the past, speculative discussion of problems by philosophers has often prepared the way for a scientific treatment of those problems. And often enough a doctrine such as atomism has been worked out, and its implications explored, by the speculative metaphysician, long before any use could be made of it in the detailed investigations of science.

(2) When we have completed and set forth our scientific conclusions, still, to know the latest findings of physics, of biology, of psychology, and set them in a row, does not give us a coherent and comprehensive picture of the world ; it gives us a series of pictures which do not coalesce into a single pattern. An interpretation of the world based on only one department of knowledge is bound to be to some extent distorted. The scientist's temptation is to think that his own particular specialism gives him the truth about the world as a whole. He propounds a physical or biological world-theory which pays too little attention to matters that are irrelevant to physics or biology. There is, then, at the least, a task of co-ordination to be done ; and in this task the philosopher must also consider the different outlooks and insights into reality provided by novelists, mystics, and moralists. All our scientists are describing the same world, but in many different languages. We must put their descriptions into a single language, which will reveal the common features of that world.

(3) All our discussion of any kind of theory, scientific or not, proceeds against a background of certain general assumptions about the nature of the world, which determine

what kind of theory seems to us plausible, and what kind of explanation acceptable. These assumptions are, at least in part, variable. They change slowly from one age to another, and it is they, rather than any particular doctrines, which give the thought of an age or a civilisation its peculiar character. Every now and then, observation discloses facts which will not square with the current assumptions ; as the nineteenth-century notion of physical causation failed to fit the facts revealed by the study of entities smaller than the atom, and ordinary present-day notions of mental causation fail to fit the facts of telepathy and clairvoyance as revealed by experiment ; and then a recasting of the assumptions is necessary. So there is need for a study which shall ferret out these assumptions and set them forth plainly—for they are largely implicit and half-conscious ; shall keep a critical eye on them, measuring them against available knowledge ; shall loosen the prejudices of its particular age, and keep open alternative ways of thinking.

Metaphysics, then, has the tasks of speculating on questions not yet soluble, of co-ordinating knowledge, and of criticising assumptions. These tasks cannot, in the nature of things, be performed with the precision and certainty which are properly expected of the scientist. The metaphysician, like the mountaineer, moves often in the clouds and with insecure foothold. But this is no argument against metaphysics. For to deprecate the discussion of metaphysical views does not prevent people from having them, it only prevents them from having thoughtful and considered views which have stood the test of argument. They will be left instead with views which are all the more likely to have their origin in prejudice or passion, or in the hasty extension to all reality of certain principles suitable to a particular aspect of it (engineering or art or worship or political propaganda). Indeed, though we may avoid discussing our metaphysical system, we can hardly avoid having one. For even if we do no more than ask a question, we may unconsciously take for granted something of importance about the nature of things. If I ask " What is

the cause of cancer ? ", I am assuming that there are general
laws of uniform causation holding among events of the type
to which cancer belongs. If I ask " What is the nature of
ultimate reality ? ", I assume that there are grades of
realities, that some of them are permanent and others
transient, some dominant and others dependent. If I ask
" What is the meaning of life ? " or " Why are we here ? ",
I assume that human life can be interpreted as though it were
the result of a design, an intention to fulfil some purpose or
other, and so I beg what is perhaps the most fundamental of
all questions in philosophy.

9.—IDEALISM AND MATERIALISM

For, amongst the immense variety of opinions and
schools of thought to be found in the history of philosophy
probably the most conspicuous and the most deeply significant
division is that between the schools of materialism and
idealism. The difference between a materialist and an
idealist type of philosophy cannot be expressed in any simple
formula. But it is, at bottom, a difference between two
kinds of explanation of the nature of things. The Idealist
believes that the world is fundamentally a purposive system
and can be explained in terms of purposes or ends or ideals
the question " What is this for ? " is for him always a valid
question, and behind the mere sequence of one event or
another, there is always a " meaning " to be discerned
The Materialist denies this, and holds that the one adequate
kind of explanation of the world is in terms of cause and
effect. Things happen as they do because they are the
necessary sequels of what went before. To understand a
situation, we must know the situation which preceded it
together with the causal laws according to which the things
in that situation behave. As to purposes and ideals, these
occur but rarely in the world, and when they do occur, are
to be accounted for as inevitable effects of preceding, purpose
less causes.

This difference is equivalent to a difference of view about the status of Mind in the universe ; for in our experience it is Mind which entertains purposes and cares for values. If we live in a fundamentally spiritual world, in which Mind is permanent and dominant, then there is reason to seek an intended, intelligible pattern in it, reason to hope that ideals not unlike our own may be cherished and pursued by the universe as a whole ; we may properly adopt an emotional attitude of reverence or of fellow-feeling towards our vast spiritual environment. But if Mind is only transient and dependent in the universe, if the things that endure and dominate are unconscious, uncomprehending, purposeless, then there is nothing to be hoped for in the fulfilment of our desires except what our own wit and strength can achieve ; the universe at large is indifferent to us and our purposes, and no emotional response to it as a whole can be appropriate. Clearly, our choice between these two philosophies may strongly influence the way we conduct our lives. And, consciously or unconsciously, we can hardly avoid choosing.

The dispute between the materialist and the idealist ways of interpreting the world will be the main subject of this book. I proceed to an examination of Materialism.

FURTHER READING.

On Rationalism and Empiricism.
R. Descartes—*Meditations* (a classic).
B. Russell—*Problems of Philosophy* (a lucid introduction).
A. J. Ayer—*Language, Truth and Logic.*
W. H. Walsh—*Metaphysics.*
H. H. Price—*Thinking and Experience.*

For another point of view :
H. Bergson—*Introduction to Metaphysics.*

II

MATERIALISM

10.—MATERIALISM AND THE SCIENTIFIC OUTLOOK

MATERIALISM is a widespread and persistent type of philosophy, because it springs naturally out of one special kind of experience which comes in some degree to all men and all ages. This is the experience which is characteristic of the craftsman, the engineer, and the scientist ; in which man studies the behaviour of the things he finds in the world about him in order to find out how they work, so that he may be able to control them and manipulate them and make them work according to his own intentions. When we try to understand other things (including other people), not in order to enjoy them or sympathise with them, admire or condemn them, but in order to alter them and make them serve our purposes, our thinking about the world will be directed into certain definite channels. We shall want to know principally what makes a certain event happen, under what conditions and by what means a desired result can be obtained or an undesired result prevented ; that is, we shall want to know the *causes* of events. For knowledge of causal laws, coupled with knowledge of particular facts, is the only kind of knowledge which is useful—that is, enables us to use other things to gain our own ends. Now one may be keenly interested in the discovery of causal laws without holding a materialist philosophy. Nevertheless, if a man investigates nature in its causal aspect with the object of being able to control it, and if this becomes his predominant point of view in thinking about the world, his philosophy will probably incline towards materialism.

This kind of outlook has been especially and increasingly common in western Europe since the seventeenth century, that is, since the beginnings of modern science ; as the

14

scientific attitude has spread, the materialist philosophy has spread with it. For materialism is characteristically a creed of the men of science and their followers, rather than of professional philosophers ; and the scientists have often held it rather as a working assumption than as an explicitly formulated philosophy. So the history of materialism is inseparable from the history of science, and especially of that branch of science which is concerned with the fundamental nature of material things, namely, physics. It is physics which gives a clear meaning to the term " matter."

Since the conception of Matter changes as scientific discovery advances, there is more than one type of materialist philosophy. The type of philosophy I shall now discuss has, I think, the best right to the name " materialism," and my choice of it will allow me to use the word in a fairly precise sense. But it is a philosophy more characteristic of the eighteenth and nineteenth centuries than of the twentieth ; and some of its doctrines would be rejected by many thinkers calling themselves Materialists. I proceed to sketch its main principles.

II.—THE UNITY OF THE WORLD

In the first place, the world is a unity. Its unity is not that of a machine or of a work of art, which consists in the co-operation of many parts towards one purpose ; it is a unity of stuff or material—the world is one because all of it is made up of similar ingredients. So Materialism may be said to have come into existence in the very first days of " philosophy," when, in the sixth century B.C., Thales of Miletus propounded the daring doctrine that " everything is water." The characteristic which made him fix upon water as the substance of the universe was presumably its remarkable variability of form. Though it is normally liquid, high temperatures will make it vaporous, and low temperatures solid, in each case altering a great many of its properties ; yet it is the same stuff which undergoes these transformations.

So the idea of Matter is essentially this : that throughout all the changes of form and quality which physical objects undergo, there is a persistent stuff which, while subject to these changes, is nevertheless the same stuff all the time. The difference between ice and steam is great, but superficial ; substantially, they are the same, as you can show by restoring the original temperature and getting your water back again. Thales' remarkable conjecture was that what is true of the great difference between ice and steam is true also of the still greater differences between water and wood, iron, clay, flesh, etc. They have different ostensible properties ; but at bottom they are the same matter taking different forms under different conditions.

But how can such a theory be the truth ? How can a thing change its properties and yet remain the same ? If ice is hard and water soft, if ice can be cut into blocks but not poured into glasses, and water can be poured into glasses but not cut into blocks, is it not a flat contradiction to say that they are the same thing ? To make Materialism a sensible theory, we must not stop at the bare assertion of identity ; we must show in what respects all things are the same, and how their sameness in some respects is compatible with their difference in others.

12.—ATOMISM

Ancient Greek speculation provided an answer. If the material of all things is the same in quality, the differences between things must be differences of quantity and arrangement ; they must consist of different amounts of the one fundamental substance, differently distributed in space. This idea was most fully worked out in the atomic theory of Leucippus and Democritus (fifth century B.C.). According to this theory, everything in the world consists of a number of small pieces of matter, called " atoms " or " indivisibles." The atoms are much too small to be perceived by the senses. They are all alike in quality, but they differ in size and shape ;

and in different things they are in different positions, with more or less of empty space between them, and they are in motion at different speeds and in different directions. These differences of the arrangement in space of one identical matter provide all the variety there is in the world.

With the Greek thinkers, these ideas were speculations with very little evidence in their support ; and the traditions which eventually prevailed in Greek philosophy were of a very different type. But modern materialism rests on an abundance of evidence provided by the investigations of the sciences. Modern physics and chemistry provide plenty of confirmation for a theory of the nature of things similar in its essentials to that propounded by Leucippus. Physicists and chemists are now able to break up into very small parts any physical object that is given them, and to re-combine these parts to make fresh wholes. It was discovered in the nineteenth century that, if the process of breaking up a material thing is carried as far as chemical methods can carry it, the resulting fragments—called " atoms "—all belong to a limited number of standard types—the ninety-odd chemical elements. All the immense variety of things in the world can be reduced to constituent parts of less than a hundred different sorts, in varying numbers and varying combinations with each other.

The twentieth century has gone further. The " atom " was misnamed ; it is not after all indivisible, but can be split up into its parts by rougher treatment than our ancestors were able to give it. Atoms of all the different elements then break up into the same kinds of constituents—electrons, protons, neutrons—exactly how many kinds of them is still matter of inquiry, but there are certainly very few, and they are the same for all kinds of material objects. There is no discoverable difference between an electron ejected from an atom of hydrogen and one ejected from an atom of copper. The differences between the elements disappear when we reach their ultimate constituents.

But, of course, to show that by breaking up a physical object in a laboratory you can get nothing out of it but protons and electrons, does not prove that nothing but protons and electrons was ever there. Water can be split up into oxygen and hydrogen, and oxygen and hydrogen re-combined to make water. But it does not strictly follow that the water *consists* of the two gases in combination. Perhaps it is simply *transformed* into them, and they are transformed back into it. To say that the chemist has at the end of his process of analysis just the same things as he had at the beginning, differently arranged, is to make an assumption. What exactly does this assumption mean, and how can it be justified ?

13.—MECHANISM

We can give meaning to it, if the properties of water can be shown to be derivable from the properties of oxygen and hydrogen in combination. We can give meaning to the assertion that all things consist of one Matter, and nothing but Matter, if the behaviour of all things can be explained by reference to the same set of principles. Here, then, is another important aspect of the materialist philosophy. If the world is made of one kind of stuff, or of a very few similar kinds, which are found in all things, then there are not a number of different sciences, each with its own separate set of principles for explaining its own department of reality, but one science only, with one set of principles which explain everything. Since chalk and cheese are made of the same matter, their behaviour, different as it appears, must be explicable in terms of the same laws of nature which express the properties of this Matter. This one science will be the science which studies the elements of things, that is, physics.

Thus, if Materialism is true, and everything consists of, say, protons and electrons and nothing else, everything which happens in the world must be explicable by the laws which describe the behaviour of protons and electrons. Ultimately, the laws of chemistry must be deducible from the laws of physics. Similarly with biology ; the living body differs from the lifeless only in the more complex arrangement of its material parts ; the atoms which compose it are the same as those which compose lifeless things, and they behave according to the same physical laws. An explanation of the nature and behaviour of complex things by reference to the nature and behaviour of their parts is called " mechanistic " ; for it is in this way that we understand the working of a machine, presuming that the parts of it will not change their nature when they are put together to form the machine. Materialism, in the sense in which I am using the word, assumes that mechanistic explanations can be given of everything that happens. The properties of every object are determined by the properties of the protons and electrons which compose it.

14.—DETERMINISM

The materialist's type of explanation may also be called " deterministic." Since all things consist of Matter, and the nature of Matter is everywhere the same, there is only one way in which a given thing can behave in given circumstances. The laws of nature do not change ; and therefore, if we know those laws, and if we also know the quantity and disposition and present state of the matter in a given region of space at a given moment, we can predict the state of affairs in that region at a later moment, except in so far as it is affected by other matter outside the region. If we knew these facts for the whole universe at any one time, we could exhibit the whole history of the universe like the working of a great machine. It goes without saying that such knowledge is impossible for us. Any physical body large enough to be of any interest to us contains far too many protons and electrons to be counted, and they are far too small to be directly observed, so that a complete and exact knowledge of any physical situation is impossible. But we can imagine a superhuman mind which possessed knowledge of this kind ; and for such a mind nothing would be unexpected or fortuitous or inexplicable. Everything would appear as a necessary consequence of the disposition of the parts of matter in space and the laws of their behaviour.

The aim of the materialist is to approach as nearly as possible to this ideal. He will try to show that water does consist of nothing but oxygen and hydrogen by showing that the properties of water can be deduced from those of oxygen and hydrogen when we know the manner in which they are combined in water. He will try to show that the human body consists of nothing but certain quantities of the chemical elements by showing that its behaviour can be worked out when we know the laws governing the behaviour of these elements, and the way they are combined in the body.

The case for Materialism is that in scientific inquiry this method of approach is successful. This does not mean that all our sciences can, as yet, be reduced to one ; we have not a sufficiently exact knowledge, either of the nature and behaviour of the ultimate constituents of matter, or of the manner in which they are combined in large-scale objects, to be able to do this. The sciences studying the more complex phenomena have to discover their own principles of explanation independently of the knowledge of simpler phenomena which is given by physics. But a vast number of laws of the mechanist, determinist type have been discovered, and more are continually being discovered as scientific investigation goes on. We can, for instance, account for the way in which things become hotter or colder by supposing that they consist of a great number of moving particles, that the hotter a thing is, the faster the movement of its particles, and that change of temperature is the result of collisions between particles, and consequent changes of their speeds. We have made more than a beginning in the reduction of chemical to physical laws by explaining the capacity of some of the chemical elements to combine with one another by reference to the structure of their atoms. We are finding out how the organs of living bodies work by breaking them down into their chemical components and applying the known laws of chemistry to them. We can explain many of the peculiarities of heredity by supposing that a particular characteristic in which individuals of a species differ from one another is the result of the presence of one minute material thing, the " gene," which occupies a definite place on a definite chromosome in the germ-cell, and that the combination of qualities an individual derives from its parents is determined by the way the germ-cells from the parents divide and join together. And so on. The most certain and exact of the findings of science are of this character, explaining wholes by reference to the properties of their parts.

15.—THE PRINCIPLE OF INDETERMINACY

Of recent years a good deal of fuss has been made over the effect on scientific philosophy of the so-called Principle of Indeterminacy, first laid down by Heisenberg and generally accepted by contemporary physicists. Some people have argued that by accepting this principle physicists have abandoned the whole idea of a deterministic mechanical universe, and adopted instead the idea of a universe in which events do not follow precisely from their causes. I think this fuss is quite unnecessary. Heisenberg showed that, with any apparatus which we possess or can conceive as physically possible, it is impossible to discover both the precise position and the precise velocity of an electron within certain margins of error : and therefore the ideal of a complete deterministic account of the universe is in principle unattainable, since we can never obtain with sufficient accuracy the primary data from which such an account must start. This discovery is of great importance for scientific procedure. But its meta-physical importance is very small. No-one ever supposed that a complete deterministic account of the world was possible in practice, or that Laplace's superhuman calculator could be made flesh and dwell among us. What the mechanistic determinists said was that every particle of matter had a determinate position and velocity, that these positions and velocities determined everything that happened in the universe, and that it was the business of the physicist to discover them as exactly as he could. Heisenberg's principle does not affect this position : the "indeterminacy" in question is the inability of the physicist to find out exactly where the electron is, it is not an inability of the electron to be exactly anywhere. It is true that twentieth-century physics, in contrast to earlier physics, has to state many of its fundamental laws in terms of statistical averages of large numbers of events. But this is no reason for supposing that the events it deals with are in any degree causeless or capricious. Insurance companies also base their calculations on statistical averages ; but this is not a reason for regarding death as a causeless phenomenon ; the reliability of the averages suggests the contrary.

16.—THE ESSENTIAL PROPERTIES OF MATTER

So far we have considered the view that the whole universe consists of one uniform stuff, but we have not inquired what kind of stuff it is. We must now ask what properties belong to the fundamental constituents of matter ; for then, presumably, we shall learn the ultimate nature of things. The answer we get is surprising. Common sense, when it sets out to describe the world, does so in terms of a great variety of sensible qualities, hot and cold, wet and dry, hard and soft, light and dark, and so on. Coal is hard, black, solid, heavy ; sugar is soft, white, sweet, etc. But in the descriptions of the world given by modern physics, no such properties appear. Atoms and electrons are not credited with colour, warmth or coldness, hardness or softness, or any properties of sound or smell or taste. They are credited with a position, and a rate and direction of motion, and with certain other properties, of which "mass," "energy," "electric charge" appear to be the chief. When we ask what these fundamental properties are and how they are ascertained, it seems that all of them are definable in terms

of *motion* : the " mass," " energy," " electric charge " of a
particle signify various propensities of that particle to move in
certain directions at certain velocities when in certain
relations to other particles, and various propensities of other
particles to move in certain ways when in certain relations
with it. Thus an essential principle of the methods of
procedure of modern physics was laid down in Galileo's
statement : " It is only possible to understand the qualitative
changes in nature when they can be traced back to
quantitative changes, which means here to motions in space."

In justification of this standpoint, two considerations
may be noted. (1) Physics seeks for those properties of
material things which they possess independently of the
conditions under which they are observed, so that different
observers, under different conditions, can agree as to what
these properties are. It is easy to see that colour, for instance,
is not such a property. The colour a thing appears to have
can be changed by changing, not the thing itself, but the
conditions under which it is observed—by drawing the
curtains and admitting the daylight, by putting on a pair
of dark glasses, by looking at it from the other end of the
room, so that light and shadow are differently distributed
over it. A colour-blind man sees no difference between what
I call " red " and what I call " green." You may say that
it is the peculiar condition of his organs of sight which
prevents him from drawing the distinction ; but it is equally
true that it is the peculiar condition of *my* organs of sight
which makes me draw it. So with warmth and coldness.
If you plunge into a bowl of lukewarm water one hand which
has just been in hot water, and one which has just been in
cold, the one hand will feel cold and the other hot ; but it is
the same water in the bowl. What are the observable
properties of material things about which all observers will
agree ? They are found to be certain spatial and temporal
properties. We can agree (with a negligible margin of error)
about certain measurements which tell us where a given thing
is, and in what direction and at what rate it has moved.

It is upon these agreed measurements that physical science is founded ; and from them its fundamental concepts are derived.

(2) Physics seeks for those properties of things which are permanent and universal, those which everything possesses all the time. Now colour, warmth, hardness, etc., are not universal and permanent properties of things. Some things are colourless, tasteless, odourless. When our piece of coal is placed on the fire, it soon loses its hardness, its blackness, and its coldness. If we are to say that the smoke and ashes to which it has been reduced are in any sense the same stuff as the original coal, we must look for other properties which are permanent. " Mass " and " energy "—or some more general property of which mass and energy are alternative forms—have been found to be such permanent properties.

The materialist philosopher takes the account given by physics as an adequate account of the nature of ultimate reality ; and so to him these fundamental physical properties are the essential properties of all that is. The rest—colour, sound, warmth, hardness, smell, and so on—the so-called " secondary qualities "—are all derivative from these universal and permanent properties of the atoms which make up the material world.

III

EPIPHENOMENALISM

17.—WHAT IS THE PLACE OF MIND IN A MATERIAL WORLD?

THAT the point of view I have been describing is the correct one in approaching the problems of physics and chemistry, and at least some of the problems of biology, no informed person now denies. Materialism embodies at least part of the truth about the world. The question at issue is whether or not it embodies the whole truth. If it is the whole truth, then a materialistic account can in principle be given, not merely of those physical and chemical processes which occur in the history of lifeless things, or are common to the lifeless and the living, but also of the history and experience of living and conscious beings. The materialist philosophy is in undisputed possession of the realm of the inorganic. But with the realms of life and of mind it is otherwise.

As to living matter, I shall not here concern myself with it further than to observe that biologists themselves are not agreed whether the notion of mechanical causation appropriate in physics and chemistry is adequate for the understanding of biological processes too, or whether it must be supplemented by special principles of causation belonging to the nature of life itself.

18.—DIFFERENCE BETWEEN MENTAL AND PHYSICAL PROPERTIES

But a still wider gulf yawns between stones and gases and light-rays on the one hand, and conscious experience on the other. It is this discordance between the characters of matter and those of mind which especially leads philosophers to doubt or deny the materialist doctrine. The difficulty is to see how conscious experience can possibly be explained according to the concepts and methods of physical science. Physics correlates motions in space with other motions in space ; and the things which move are very small quantities of a uniform stuff. But a mind is not a movement, or a collection of movements, in space. Indeed, it appears to have no spatial properties at all. If it had, presumably my opinion that it is going to rain would be larger or smaller than, to the left or to the right of, my feeling of annoyance ; which seems absurd. Moreover, my mind does not consist of atoms or any such constituents. While it is possible to analyse a mind and distinguish in it various sensations, feelings, thoughts, and again various impulses, desires, purposes, it is not possible to discern in it anything which at all fills the place of an atom or electron in the physical account of the world. How then can the theory of Matter throw any light on this entirely different mental order of reality ?

If Materialism means that the entities and properties dealt with by physics are the *sole* realities in the world, if it means, in Hobbes' downright phrase, " All that exists is body, all that occurs motion," then it can hardly escape absurdity. For conscious experience simply does not have the properties of spatiality, mobility, atomicity, attributed by physics to the matter which it studies ; even if it be supposed to have them, it certainly has other properties which cannot be reduced to these. To say, with Hobbes, that pleasure *is* but motion about the heart, or, with Bradlaugh, that conscience *is* a spasm of the diaphragm, is, if the words are meant literally, just nonsense. For the difference between joy and sorrow, between thinking of your breakfast and thinking of the policy of the government, is not a difference of spatial position, faster and slower, greater or less mass or energy, or any combination of these. There is no doubt that atomic and mechanistic theories can account for the motions of bodies in space ; but special reasons are evidently required for supposing that such theories can also explain a different

kind of event, namely, experience. The problem arises :
What is the relation between the experiences of conscious
beings and the movements in space of measurable quantities
of " mass " and " energy " and " electric charge " ?

19.—PROBLEM OF "SECONDARY QUALITIES"

It is not merely in respect of such evidently " mental "
operations as loving and hating, rejoicing and sorrowing,
that the problem must be raised. It concerns the whole
range of so-called " secondary " qualities, redness and
greenness and shrillness and smoothness and sweetness and
so on. For, as we have seen, physics does not attribute any
of these properties to its material reality. The dance of the
electrons around their nucleus is a colourless, tasteless,
soundless performance. Yet these properties are not expelled
from reality by labelling them " secondary " ; the colour
blue certainly exists, for we can see it, and the fragrance of
roses, for we can smell it. But they do not belong to the
material world of physics. What then do they belong to ?
The men who fixed the outlines of the standard philosophy
of physics up till recent years answered with some confidence
' To the mind." The secondary qualities are said to arise
in consciousness, when a mind becomes aware of the world
around it. They belong to consciousness, for we are aware
of them in sensation. But they do not belong to that world
outside of and distinct from consciousness with which physics
is concerned. Thus the development of physics has
aggravated and intensified the problem of Mind and Body
by stripping the material object of all those qualities which
make up the content of our sense-perception, and are
attributed by common sense to an external reality. If the
physicists' account of the external world is true and adequate,
then what we perceive is not that world, nor even an accurate
copy of it, but a misleading appearance. The materialist
philosopher, if he accepts this account of the matter, must
deny that anything present in our experience forms part of the

physical world. Believing, as he does, that there is only one world, he is faced with a formidable task in remedying this " bifurcation of nature." How is he to re-unite the internal and external realities so sharply sundered by his meagre conception of the ultimate nature of things ?

20.—EPIPHENOMENALISM

His solution of the problem runs along lines like these. Consciousness is a reality indeed, but it is not an independent or ultimate reality. Consciousness is a property of certain complex material objects—namely, animal organisms. It is not an essential and fundamental property of matter, but a derivative property which matter acquires or produces under certain rather peculiar conditions, when it is arranged in certain rare and special ways. Occasionally a material system, having got into an unusually complex sort of arrangement, becomes conscious, and remains so just as long as this complex arrangement continues. When the arrangement of material particles is broken up and replaced by another arrangement, consciousness ceases, while the permanent attributes of matter remain.

Every conscious being (" mind " or " soul " or "person") is also a material being ; and he is material primarily, and mental only in the second place. That is to say, his nature as a mental being is completely determined by his nature as a material being. The movements of masses in space, which are the causes of everything else in the world, also cause the states of consciousness of men and other animals. The atoms move, and a certain state of consciousness supervenes. Thus, if we knew the exact disposition of the atoms of all the substances in a man's body, we could know by means of the laws of physics and chemistry exactly how he would behave, without any need for independent knowledge of what was passing in his " mind." Physical influences give a complete explanation of everything which goes on in the body ; and of these bodily processes the mental processes are a mere appendage, reflection, or, as some thinkers of this school have said, " epiphenomenon " (something which appears on top of or in addition to Matter) ; whence the theory that mental processes are entirely determined by physical processes is sometimes called Epiphenomenalism.

On this theory sensation is the consciousness of what is happening in the body as it is stimulated by other bodies. Desire is the consciousness of certain impulses and tensions in the nervous system. Emotion is the consciousness of the effects on the brain of increased or reduced activity of the glands, etc. The mind observes what is being done, but is not in any proper sense the doer of anything. It is the material forces, acting according to the same principles and in the same manner in a human body as in any other piece of matter, which are the real agents. The difference between living things and dead things is great ; but it is not a difference of ultimate nature ; it is merely a difference in complexity of arrangement.

It follows that the way to understand human nature, experience and conduct, fully and completely, is through the understanding of its fundamental causes, which are physical processes. A scientific knowledge of mankind can come only through the study of the nature and operations of the human body, i.e., through physiology. At present, indeed, physiology is not sufficiently advanced to be able to tell us much about the detailed workings of those bodily processes which are accompanied by consciousness. So our knowledge of human experience and conduct is not yet properly scientific ; it is still on the level of rough-and-ready common-sense generalisation.

Psychologists have to rely for much of their inform- ation on introspection, on the accounts which men give of what passes through their consciousness. They examine the characteristics, tendencies, and patterns which can be discerned in consciousness. But this method of study can never do more than scratch the surface of the problems of human nature, arriving at precarious generalisations coloured

by individual bias. For in examining conscious experience
we are studying the superficial and not the fundamental
facts, the effects and not their underlying causes. The
effects may appear simple, but the causes are highly complex
and elaborately interrelated. Since many of the physical
processes which determine experience are outside the reach
of consciousness altogether, introspection will never give us
the whole story, but only fragmentary glimpses, from which
we can never derive a connected understanding of the whole
matter.

At present, a science of the human body, which will at
the same time explain the workings of the soul, is a hope and
not an achievement. What reasons can be given by materialist
philosophers for entertaining this hope ? Why should the
concepts and laws of physics ultimately comprehend mental
as well as physical phenomena ? The most important
arguments for this conclusion can be brought together under
three heads.

21.—ARGUMENT FROM THE CONTINUITY OF NATURE

The first I will call the argument from the continuity of
nature. The materialist case is that all nature is formed of
one stuff, and the mental is a quality or phase or aspect of
that stuff. There are no absolute distinctions or unbridgeable
gulfs between one group of natural objects and another.

This view finds confirmation in what we know of the
history of life on the earth. The experts in the matter are
agreed that for the greater part of its history the earth has
contained no living creatures, but only masses of inorganic
matter. When living things did eventually appear, they took
forms which were extremely simple in comparison with those
which now exist. As one living thing gave birth to another,
a greater variety and complexity in plant and animal life
came about. By slow stages, by small variations from one
generation to another, the large, elaborate, complex living
creatures of our own era came into being. Thus, within the

kingdom of the living, there appears to be a complete continuity of development, each creature differing only a little from its ancestors. Living creatures are members of a single related stock. Men are the direct descendants of creatures who, in the form of their bodies and brains, in the kind of life they lived, and, we may presume, in their mental characteristics too, were similar to present-day apes ; the line of descent passes through intermediate forms, neither clearly human nor clearly simian. The apes in their turn are linked with many other species of animals, perhaps in the end with them all. A line drawn through this biological succession to mark off men from apes, or higher animals from lower, would have to be as arbitrary as a line marking off " white " men from " coloured."

And as there is continuity in descent, so there is continuity in type and characteristics. Certainly, there are differences between men and other animals ; certainly, there are innumerable things which men can do and animals cannot, as well as things which they can do and we cannot. But these differences can still be interpreted as differences of degree ; we possess the same capacities as our humbler relatives, but in a more highly developed form. It used to be argued that " reason " was a power altogether different in kind from any animal capacity, and confined, on earth, to men. But careful observation of our nearest animal relatives has clearly shown that they possess, in a smaller degree than ourselves, the capacity to work out a problem, to plan a course of action, to envisage a state of affairs not yet actual— that is, to " reason " in any fair sense of the word.*

We shall reach the same result if we consider the history of the individual human being. However much we may argue over the evidence of our descent from ape-like ancestors, there is no doubt that each one of us is immediately descended from a living creature of a much more primitive kind than any ape—namely, a spermatozoon. The growth of a human individual begins with the junction of two tiny cells, forming

*See for instance Köhler *Mentality of Apes*.

an organism which lacks almost all of the distinguishing characteristics of humanity ; and the development from the embryo to the adult is gradual, so that there is no point at which one can say definitely that a human personality comes into existence.

As there is continuity between different species of animals, so there are similarities between animals and plants ; both are cell-complexes, sharing certain fundamental processes of life. There are some intermediate types of creature which biologists hesitate whether to classify as animal or plant.

But what are we to say of the wider and deeper differences between living organisms of all kinds and non-living, inorganic matter ? Here the materialist can plausibly argue : " If at first there was only inorganic matter, and then there appeared very simple organisms, later more complex organisms, is it not reasonable to suppose that the original simple organisms were developed out of the inorganic material, just as the later complex organisms were developed out of the simple ones ? For we find that the constituents of the most complex living bodies are the very same chemical elements which are found in inorganic matter. There is no material to be found in the living which was not present at the beginning in the lifeless ; and there is no source discoverable from which life might have originated, except this lifeless matter. We know that, in the production of living creatures, these inorganic materials are needed, and that they can be converted into organic form ; this conversion is being perpetually accomplished by the plants. We have no trace of any other ingredient or agency needed to produce a living and conscious being except these inorganic materials. We can then reasonably conclude that the living creature consists simply of the inorganic ingredients in a somewhat peculiar form, the maintenance of which form is life, and its loss death.

The derivation of the living from the lifeless would be proved if we were able to construct a living body artificially out of inorganic materials. This we cannot yet do. We can produce artificially some peculiar and elaborate chemical compounds which in nature are to be found only in living bodies. But on earth at present, all life is from the living. We must therefore suppose that the production of the first living things took place under highly unusual circumstances— perhaps entirely unique circumstances, for there is no good evidence for the existence of life anywhere else in the universe except on the earth. We do not know what these unusual circumstances were ; but we have no reason for doubting that they were physical and chemical in nature."

22.—CRITICISM OF THIS ARGUMENT

I must now try to assess the force of this line of argument. It seems to me to work very strongly against Radical Dualism, the kind of theory which asserts an absolute discrepancy between Nature and Mind, and supposes a sudden irruption of an alien influence into the material world. If Mind, in the form in which we know it, is an eternal reality, self-subsistent, independent of Matter, why is it that for so many ages in the earth's history there is no trace whatever of its presence and activity ? And if it is not eternal, but produced, what can have produced it but that which alone we know to have been here before it, namely, inorganic matter ? The reasonable view on the evidence appears to be that living and conscious things are sprung from lifeless and unconscious things, and the " higher " living things from the " lower," just as in the individual there is a development from less to more elaborate forms of life and of experience.

In the beginning, then, was the lifeless, and the lifeless of itself took on the form of the living. Can we then say that the living is nothing but the lifeless in a more complicated form ? I do not think we can. To justify such a way of speaking, we should have to assume that all change in the world is merely the re-arrangement of existing material ; that nothing is ever created or destroyed ; that there is no genuine novelty in the world ; and so, what exists at the end of a process must be the same as what existed at the beginning of it. Unless you assume this, you cannot show that a complex living body is nothing more than its physical material arranged in a particular way.

But if you do make such an assumption, then you can stand the argument on its head and make it yield a precisely opposite conclusion. If there is no genuine novelty in the world, if what exists now is simply the re-arrangement of what has existed always, then, since the world now contains scientific insight, æsthetic enjoyment, personal affection, and other characteristics of highly-developed minds, these characteristics must always have been present in the universe, either hidden in inorganic matter itself, or in the mind of God or some other being or beings distinct from matter.

If we make the assumption that whatever is real must be eternal, I think this second line of argument somewhat more convincing than the first. But I am not prepared to accept either of them, for I see no good reason for accepting the common assumption on which both of them are based. It is true that there is at least one factor or feature in nature which is permanent and unchanging, namely, that which corresponds to the physicist's measurements of mass and energy. But other features are variable ; the permanence of mass-energy is quite compatible with the variability of other characters of things. And, because a character is permanent, it does not at all follow that it is more " real " or more influential than the variable characters.

Thus, besides the possibility that Mind is an entirely independent form of reality, and the possibility that it is merely a temporary accident of a basically real Matter, there is a third alternative, quite compatible with the scientific facts which have just been summarised. This is that Mind is indeed a comparative novelty in the history of the world, and has come into being as the result of a process taking place in inorganic matter ; but yet it does contain unique characters which do not belong to the inorganic matter out of which it arose, and which could not be forecast on the basis of any knowledge of the behaviour of matter when unorganised. It would then not be the case, even in principle, that we could reduce all the laws of biology and psychology to those of physics and chemistry. Nor would it be the case that only the physical properties of matter are effective in nature. We can admit that mental states originated from non-mental states, without admitting that, once they have come into being, they are impotent to determine the course of the world's history. Sprung from Matter, we may yet become its masters.

This third alternative type of theory, then, rejects the principle of mechanical determinism, that a whole can be no more than the sum of its parts. It supposes that a molecule in a living body may acquire other properties and behave in other ways than could possibly be deduced from its properties and behaviour in inorganic environments. In this case there would be, in a sense, different levels of reality, and different stages of development, in the history of the world.

We may, then, admit that living organisms, with their characteristic of consciousness and all that goes with it, have been produced by inorganic matter without external assistance, and at the same time hold that the peculiar characteristics of conscious beings are causally operative in the process of nature, and are not purely effects or shadows of the material.

23.—ARGUMENT THAT A NON-PHYSICAL CAUSE CANNOT HAVE PHYSICAL EFFECTS

But here we must meet another kind of argument on which materialists often rely ; namely, the difficulty of discovering, or even conceiving, how conscious mind can produce any effect on the material world with which it is implicated. It is argued : " The physical world, according to our knowledge of it (which is by far the most extensive and accurate knowledge we have of anything) is governed by a fairly small number of fairly simple laws, whereby from one physical state another physical state follows without fail. The laws of physics and chemistry appear to extend throughout the whole realm of matter, making it one realm with one consistent mode of action. Now, the human body is a part of this realm, and its parts, therefore, obey the laws of physics and chemistry. This might have been expected in advance, from the fact that the human body consists of the same kind of stuff as everything else ; and it is in fact confirmed by all the observations we are able to make on the manner of its working. As a physical body, the human organism behaves like other physical bodies.

It is not very easy to find out how the various complex chemical processes of a living body proceed ; for, if you cut a man open to see how he works, you are liable to find that your inquisitiveness has destroyed your specimen ; but wherever we can get adequate verification, we find that the laws of chemical change are just the same inside the living body as outside it ; we have no evidence of their being broken. The great principle of the conservation of energy seems to be observed in the living body as well as everywhere else ; the intake of energy is balanced by the output of work within the probable margin of error of observation.

But if the material world forms a self-contained system operating according to definite and invariable laws, then every action and passion of the human body must be completely determined by the forces of that system, and there is no room whatever for the intervention of any force other than a material one. For any such intervention would be bound to break the laws of nature ; and there is no evidence that the laws of nature are ever broken in this fashion, and plenty of evidence that they are observed. If the physical and chemical conditions thus completely determine everything that happens to a human body, there is nothing for any non-physical determinant, such as a conscious mind, to do. The mind must be a passenger, entirely without influence on the stream of events which it contemplates.

How indeed is it possible that an immaterial thing, possessing no physical energy of any kind, can nevertheless produce physical effects? How can it do the work which could otherwise only be done by physical things possessing definite quantities of physical energy and producing results proportionate to the expenditure of that energy? Such an intervention of mind into the course of nature must be miraculous; science could not deal with it or understand it. No method is suggested by which this passage of causal influence from one kind of entity to another wholly different kind of entity could take place; no laws of its operation can be guessed at. The whole alleged influence of mind on body is, from the scientific point of view, a mysterious anomaly."

24.—CRITICISM OF THIS ARGUMENT

This argument looks at first sight more formidable than it really is. We know very little about the manner in which mind can influence body, and are quite unable to imagine how this influence becomes effective. But our inability to imagine it does nothing to show that it does not happen. Nobody nowadays claims to be able to imagine the events which take place in the interior of the atom; but beyond doubt there are such events, and their effects outside the atom are discernible. It is not important whether we can imagine the interaction of mind and body in the way in which we can imagine a collision between two billiard-balls. What is important is whether we have good reason to believe that this interaction takes place.

It is true that there have been philosophers who maintained it as a self-evident truth that a cause must resemble its effect; but it is not. A draught is not much like a cold in the head; and there is no *a priori* reason why motion should not be produced by something which is not motion.

And this argument, like the preceding one, has the effect of a boomerang. For the materialist, while he denies the causal action of mind upon matter, must assert the causal action of matter upon mind. And this (the causing by motion of something which is not motion) is just as much an anomaly in the system of nature as the opposite process. For we should then have in nature an effect which was not a cause, a one-way traffic in causal connexion just as much at variance with scientific principles as the two-way traffic which dualists assume.

The fact is, physics cannot deal with mental phenomena as such. In whichever way they are introduced into material nature, they are anomalies, and can find no satisfactory place there. An influence of mind upon body would indeed be " miraculous " in the sense of being something not accounted for by physical laws or describable in physical terms. But all that this means is that the laws of physics may not be the whole truth about the universe. And it has yet to be proved that they are.

IV

MIND AND BRAIN

25.—PARALLELS BETWEEN MIND AND BRAIN

HOW can this be shown ? The final test of the epiphenomenalist theory must be its ability to interpret and account for the phenomena of consciousness by reference to material causes, by showing, for each kind of mental state, some kind of bodily state on which it depends. If Epiphenomenalism is true, then to all changes in a person's state of mind, there must correspond changes in the state of his body which are their causes. If, on the other hand, the mind is an independent thing operating according to its own laws or its own arbitrary will, then we may very well expect to find mental operations carried on independently of matter, having no material counterpart ; we may expect to find that different states of mind may accompany the same state of body, and conversely. If it can be shown that conscious experiences of a given kind occur only in the presence of material processes of a given kind, we may safely conclude that consciousness is not a separate and independent order of happenings in nature, that there are not two realms of being but only one, proceeding according to one set of principles. The materialist therefore seeks to show that this parallel holds good. Let us look at his evidence.

First, as far as our experience goes, mental processes occur only in association with physical processes, and with physical processes of a very peculiar kind. For a living organism is a rare and unusual kind of material object even on the earth, still more in the universe at large ; nor is it by any means all living bodies which give evidence of the occurrence of mental processes ; plants do not, and we may well hesitate to attribute anything worth calling " mind " to the more primitive animal types—worms, for instance. It is only the most complex types of animals which exhibit unmistakable mentality. Among these, too, there is considerable variation in the ability to perceive, to learn, and to think.

Now wherever we find clear evidence of the occurrence of mental processes, there also we find a peculiar kind of physical structure, namely, an elaborate nervous system centred upon a brain. Wherever we find evidence of the more elaborate and refined mental processes, there we find unusually large and complex brains ; and, roughly speaking, the greater the mental capacity, the larger and more complex the brain (relatively to the size of the animal). It appears, not only that there are no minds without living organisms, but that there are none but very rudimentary mental processes without brain processes in partnership.

It is not merely the possession of a brain that matters, but the right kind of brain in the right kind of condition. As the mental powers of a child grow, so its brain grows, both in size, and in the complexity of connexions between the nerve-fibres which compose it. If the brain fails to develop, the child does not learn, just as, if its legs do not grow, it cannot walk. It looks as though the brain does the learning in the way that the legs do the walking. The development continues into old age. Then we find that the brain-substance is no longer able to form new connexions of nerves ; and at the same time we find that the mind is no longer able to acquire fresh knowledge and skill. Insanity and feeble-mindedness are often found to accompany abnormalities in the structure and the electrical rhythms of the brain.

The brain does not work by itself, in spontaneous independence of its material environment. A good whiff of chloroform will forthwith put a stop, not merely to the more advanced mental processes, but to all consciousness whatever. A sufficiency of alcohol will slow down and confuse thought (this is in virtue of effects on the blood-stream carried to the brain ; a drunkard's unsteadiness is not in his legs, but in his head). What can be the explanation of facts like these, if not that the mind or soul is a function of the condition of the brain ? If mind or soul were a separate entity, why should its awareness be abolished by a whiff of chloroform or a blow on the back of the head ?

If mental life *is* a function of the physical activity of the brain, it should be possible to find out which particular conditions of the brain are responsible for particular processes of consciousness. To some extent this has been done. Our knowledge of the correlations between brain-state and mind-state is recent, but is quite rapidly increasing. It is established that sensation occurs only when the appropriate areas of the brain are stimulated—different areas for the different senses ; and the nature of the sensation—red or blue, sweet or bitter, soft or loud, etc.—varies according to the nature of the stimulation. It is established that the destruction or injury of certain parts of the brain destroys or injures the ability to remember and recognise certain kinds of things—written words, for instance.

The evidence does not prove that there is a perfect and exact correspondence between the state of the brain and the state of the mind. It shows that there is, for instance, an association between the ability to remember written words and the condition of a special area of the brain ; it does not show that there is a special condition of the brain corresponding to remembering the word " cat," and another for the word " dog." This precise detailed correspondence is as yet a hypothesis ; but it is a plausible hypothesis, which is constantly receiving fresh confirmation, especially in regard to perception.

Nor does the evidence show that the mental process and the brain process are like each other ; rather the opposite. What corresponds to the difference between red and blue in sensation is not redness and blueness in the brain, but a difference of pattern in the electrical processes taking place there. What corresponds to the single visual image in consciousness when I look at something is *two* separate patterns of nervous vibration in different parts of the brain. The mind does not, apparently, copy or " mirror " what takes place in the brain ; it seems to accompany the physical process with a process of its own which varies with the physical process, but has different qualities.

26.—CONCLUSIONS FROM THESE PARALLELS

These facts afford evidence against the separateness and independence of the mind or soul. They make it improbable that there are any purely mental operations in which the brain is not concerned. They make it probable that there is a causal connection between states of mind and states of body. But, by themselves, they cannot tell us which way these causal connections run.

The correlations could exist (*a*) if the brain-state determined the mind-state, or (*b*) if the mind-state determined the brain-state, or (*c*) if both mental and physical causes were operative at each stage of the process, jointly determining both mental and physical effects. We cannot show directly which of these three alternatives is correct. For, even if we had sufficiently detailed knowledge of the brain-state (which we have not), we could never discover which of the processes was first in time, since we have no means of dating the mental process independently of the physical.

But there are some strong considerations in favour of the materialist account of the matter. In the case which we know most about, namely, sensation, the temporal and causal priority seems to belong quite plainly to the physical process. For here the brain-state in question is the effect of a chain of physical causes which we can trace throughout, beginning outside the body with the emission of waves of light or sound, and continuing through the stimulation of nerves in the body up to the brain. The nerves respond physically to a physical stimulus, and the whole business proceeds according to physical principles ; while the resulting brain-state and the sensation associated with it vary in accordance with variations

n the original light-waves or sound-waves, over which the
mind has no control. Here the primacy clearly belongs to the
physical ; for the physical system is separate and independent
of mind, while the mental system cannot be shown to be
separate and independent of body.

The majority of the established correlations are cases of
this kind, where *independent* physical causes of the brain-state
can be traced, and the whole process explained in physical
terms without reference to the mind. This is true of many
events inside as well as outside the body—e.g., the secretions
of the glands are a matter of ordinary chemistry, and the
conscious mind does not intervene in them at all. So, if there
is any causal influence of mind on body, it would seem to be
limited in extent, and a good deal less striking than the
influence of body on mind.

All the same, first impressions suggest that some cases of
such influence occur. In voluntary decision—when I decide
to go for a walk, and my legs are then moved (according to
the physiologists, in response to impulses from the brain) ;
when I work out a problem " in my head," and, having
reached the solution, utter it in words ; and in some
involuntary cases, as when, worrying over a difficulty, I
produce a nervous tension and give myself indigestion ; in
such cases we feel sure that the initiative comes from the
mind, and the body follows its lead or obeys its will. This
initiative or causal effectiveness of the will presents itself as a
direct datum of consciousness as clear and evident as any
sensation, and not to be argued away by any metaphysical
theory. Can it be reasonably denied that here the mind
influences the body ? It can.

27.—HAVE WE DIRECT AWARENESS OF THE INFLUENCE
OF MIND ON MATTER ?

The materialist has first to undermine our confidence
in our direct awareness of our own causal activity. One
weakness in the grounds of this confidence was pointed out
long ago by Hume.* I am supposed to know, by a direct

*Inquiry concerning Human Understanding, Sec. VII.

inspection of the experience, that my decision to move my leg is the direct cause of my leg's moving. But the moving of a leg is a very complicated process. It involves the transmitting of impulses from the brain through numerous nerves to the muscles, and the setting in action of an extremely intricate series of expansions and contractions of the muscles, before the leg can be moved. The number of cells involved in the whole transaction runs into thousands, and the cell is by no means the smallest physical unit concerned. Between the initiation of the movement in the brain, and its completion in the leg, there is a long chain of nervous and muscular processes all of which are quite essential intermediaries ; unless they take place the leg does not move.

Now of these intermediate processes I have absolutely no awareness ; unless I am a student of physiology I have no idea that they take place at all. But if I am ignorant and unaware of these essential stages in the causal process, if I do not know what is really taking place, how can I possibly know that my decision or effort caused my leg to move ? If I claim to know that my act of will immediately or by itself caused the movement of my leg, my claim cannot be admitted.

Indeed, if I did know directly what sort of voluntary effort produced what sort of result, I should be freed from the necessity of learning to walk, to talk, to play the fiddle, to drive a car, etc. When we examine our experience in learning these and similar skills, we find that our procedure is pretty much the same as when we are learning about causal processes in other things : we make an effort, and then examine what has happened in order to find out precisely what we have been doing ; and we cannot unerringly distinguish the effects of our own actions from those of other causes which interfere with us, until we have had a good deal of experience of the particular kind of activity in question. (Was it, for instance, a maladroit movement of my hand which caused the car to swerve, or a defect in the steering-gear ? The case of moving my leg is in principle the same as the case of driving my car.)

I am, then, conscious of a decision or an effort ; I observe the visible or tangible movement of the leg ; but the causal connection between them, involving as it does an immense number of transmissions of current along nerves, etc., I am not and cannot be conscious of. But if I do not know *how* X causes Y, how can I know *that* X causes Y ? Surely, only in the indirect manner in which I come to know that standing in a draught causes a cold—by finding that the one is regularly followed by the other.

This doubt whether the introspective awareness of the sequence of experiences gives any real insight into their causal relations is reinforced by some of the findings of psychologists. We think that our decisions are caused by desires which are present to consciousness when we decide. But the psychologists insist that the real causes of many of our voluntary actions are " repressed " desires of which we are not aware. The conscious thoughts and feelings which seem to be our motives are only masks assumed by the real agents, which are hidden from view. It seems that introspection is not to be trusted, even as regards causal relations within the mind itself. The way is therefore open for another interpretation of the sequence of events.

28.—MIND AND BRAIN—THE EPIPHENOMENALIST THEORY

The alternative suggested by the epiphenomenalist is this. The brain, being a physical object, is linked by ordinary physical relations with the rest of the body, and so more remotely with the rest of the physical world, and these relations determine its behaviour. Each brain process is caused by other physical processes in its neighbourhood, and affects them in its turn. But brain processes (or some of them) have the peculiarity that they are accompanied by mental processes which in some way parallel or reflect them. Every mental process accompanies a brain process ; and its character is completely determined by the physical properties of this brain process, and not at all by the character of the other mental processes which precede it. The earlier stages of a train of thought, as states of consciousness, make no difference to its later stages. Thus the causes of " states of mind " are not known to introspection. They may be indirectly discovered by means of the science of physiology. As to my actions, a movement of the leg is a physical process, and so is the speech with which I announce the conclusion of a train of thought ; both of them are caused by other physical processes according to physical laws.

Without doubt it is a bold paradox to suggest that the earlier stages of a process of consciousness exert no influence on the later stages. Surely, when, for instance, I feel frightened, and cower or run or flinch, my feeling frightened is the cause of my cowering or running or flinching, and if I had not felt frightened I should not have done so ? Surely when I reach a conclusion or a decision after having thought about the matter, it is as a result of having thought, and if I had not so thought I should not have so concluded or decided ?

29.—REFLEX ACTION

But is this so certain after all ? Have you never been faced with a sudden dangerous situation, and made the appropriate response of avoidance, and only then, after having acted, begun to feel fear, and realised that you have just been in danger ? If a projectile rapidly approaches my eyes, I blink. This blinking is not a voluntary action ; I do not first decide that blinking is called for, and then blink. What happens is that I realise that I have blinked, and only then, in the same apprehension, realise that some object was approaching my eyes before I blinked. Now we already know a good deal about the physiology of processes of this kind. We know that there is a direct link between the nerves which carry the stimulation produced in the eye by the approaching object, and the nerves which carry the stimulation that makes the eyelids close, so that the stimulation of

he in-going or " afferent " nerves of itself produces a
timulation of the out-going or " efferent " nerves, and thus
he closing of the eyelids. The nerve-connection does not
pass through the brain, but through the spinal cord. This
pecific connection between particular afferent nerves,
concerned with perception, and particular efferent nerves,
concerned with motor response, is called a reflex arc ; and
his automatic type of action, which does not involve brain or
consciousness at all, is called reflex action. Reflex actions
make up a substantial part of our behaviour.

Now the brain is somewhat similar in structure to the
pattern of reflex arcs meeting in the spinal cord. The brain
also consists of afferent nerves which are connected with
efferent nerves. The difference is that the system of interconnections is immensely more complicated, the afferent
nerves being connected, not to one or a few efferent nerves, but
to an intricate network of many such. To this greater
complication of the nerve-connections in the brain corresponds
a greater complication of the actions which originate in the
brain, as compared with simple reflexes. The brain responds
in a very complex fashion to a great number of stimuli,
instead of responding in a stereotyped fashion to one small
group of stimuli. But, argues the Epiphenomenalist, the
greater complication need not mean an entire difference of
principle. The brain looks like a very complex pattern of
reflex arcs. Why, then, should we not suppose that the
mechanism of the more complex actions (which are usually
accompanied by conscious thought) is the same as the
mechanism of the simpler reflex actions which are not so
accompanied—viz., the transfer of stimulation from a group
of afferent nerves to a group of efferent nerves whose combined
action forms the total response of the organism to this complex
of stimuli ? If this is so, then we can understand why the
conscious responses of the organism (those associated with the
state of the brain) are so much more elaborate than those
performed reflexly through the spinal cord without the
accompaniment of consciousness ; for they correspond to a

much more elaborate connection of nerve-paths. The number of possible variations of response is enormously greater ; the response is not to a single stimulus of a uniform type, but to a whole mass of different sensory stimuli, which are never precisely the same on two different occasions.

We can also understand to some extent the illusion that the processes of consciousness are causally effective ; for, since the operation of the nervous system proceeds according to regular uniformities, long habituation has made it seem inevitable to us that a particular state of mind (say, feeling hungry) should be regularly followed by a particular action (say, going to the pantry). It is indeed so ; not because the one is the cause of the other, but because they are collateral effects of the same physical causes.

30.—COMPLEXITY OF UNCONSCIOUS BODILY ACTIVITY

It still comes very hard to us to believe that, complex as the nervous system is, it is capable of producing in a purely mechanical manner all the manifold achievements and ingenuities of the immense variety of human personalities. The complexity and versatility of the human machine must far surpass that of any manufactured machine we can possibly imagine. But before we dismiss this hypothesis as far-fetched, let us reflect carefully on some of the things the body can do without the aid of consciousness. Let us remember how elaborately, and yet precisely, with what extraordinary fidelity to the ancestral model, ovum and spermatozoon build themselves up from next to nothing, from dimensions below the level of the humanly visible, to a complete human body ; how silently, blindly, unobtrusively, all our organic life is steadily maintained, day in, day out ; how our food is digested and converted into flesh and bone in innumerable miniature laboratories ; how our temperature is maintained, despite the vagaries of the weather, within those narrow limits which alone allow us to carry on normal existence. Is there anything in this less complex or difficult than anything the conscious mind can claim to do ? Let us consider how a sleepwalker can in entire unconsciousness, undirected by forethought, get up, dress himself, walk downstairs, open drawers, etc.

31.—THE "UNCONSCIOUS MIND"

Ah well, you say, but this is the work, if not of the conscious mind, then of the unconscious mind. But what is this " unconscious mind " of which psychologists talk so casually, and laymen with such awe ? In the ordinary use of the word, " mind " means something conscious—feelings, desires, thoughts, all of them modes of awareness. According to this ordinary use of language, " unconscious mind " is a contradiction in terms. What is a conscious feeling, desire, or thought, we understand well enough ; what an unconscious feeling, desire, or thought could possibly be, we cannot understand at all. " The Unconscious " is indeed quite properly shrouded with an air of mystery and wonder. For it is not a familiar object we can describe, nor even an extension of something familiar into an unfamiliar field. It is not a description of something we might well recognize if we came across it. It is a mere word, a name for something which is presumably there, but whose nature we can by no means clearly conceive.

This is not to suggest that " the Unconscious " is a fiction, or to deny that psychologists have very good reasons for supposing that it exists, and for attributing to it the effects which they do attribute. But what can we reasonably suppose to exist to which these actions can be assigned ? We have reason to believe that there occur, outside consciousness, processes in some way similar to the conscious processes which we call perceiving, desiring, thinking ; processes which produce effects in our experience similar to the effects (or supposed effects) of these conscious processes. There is good evidence that something rather like desiring and thinking goes on continuously while I am not attending to it, and even while I am completely unconscious. What sort of thing can it be ?

May it not be simply the operations of the brain, the nervous system, and the rest of the body ? We have seen reason to believe that it is essentially the brain which thinks, and that desire is the physical pressure of nervous impulses tending to issue in action. Here, then, argues the materialist, here, in the continuous activity of the nervous system, is the permanent foundation on which conscious experience is only a flimsy and fragmentary superstructure. Here, in the incessant activities, interconnections, pressures, of the body, is the likeliest place to look in order to find the " unconscious," those desires, feelings, and thoughts which, without being conscious, are nevertheless real. Is it not more reasonable to attribute to the body the capacity to do unconsciously what we know that it can do consciously, rather than to invent an utterly unknown, undiscoverable, and unimaginable " unconscious mind " to do all over again what is being quite efficiently done already ?

32.—UNITY OF MIND AND BODY

For if Mind were an intruder into the material realm, of a different nature, aims, and habits, we should expect to find that its intrusion made a difference of fundamental principle to the operations of Matter ; we should expect to find that the mode of working of the mindless body was altogether different from that of the body tenanted and directed by mind. But what we do find is something different : it is that mind and body, the one consciously directing its activities, the other working in the dark, are doing much the same things in much the same way. The plant assimilates nourishment from the soil and the sunlight to grow and maintain its own living rhythm and form. The animal body, in sleep and in its manifold unconscious operations, pursues the same kind of activity, the conversion of alien matter into parts of itself. When it awakens into consciousness, it still does the same kind of thing, but more elaborately and by more roundabout methods. As the plant reaches towards the sun, the baby, impelled by the same type of fundamental drive, reaches towards the breast. When I form the conscious decision to go into a canteen and order a plate of fish and chips, does my soul then impose a new kind of activity and aim upon my living body? Or am I just making a physical response, more elaborate than the baby's, to a physical stimulus arising from a physical requirement? And the difference between going to the canteen to provide myself with food, and going to a university to provide myself with the qualifications for a job, is, in the materialist's view, only a difference of complexity. The conscious animal pursues its aim—the maintenance of its characteristic life—by more elaborate and ingenious methods than other living things, especially if it has a well-developed brain ; but after all, it is to the physical stimulus, to the imperative cry of " the body," that the conscious self responds.

If, then, the original impulse is physical, if the eventual outcome is a physical movement ending in the establishment of a physical equilibrium, what does the mind contribute to the business? The body feeds, runs, makes love, perceives, remembers. What is there left for the soul to do? What is its peculiar contribution?

Life? But plants and sleeping men live, and most of the vital processes in a man are involuntary.

Learning? But the acquisition of habits is a physical process. The memory of a piece of music is in the hands and the brain, not in the " mind," and when it is thoroughly learned, there is an automatic and thoughtless correlation between seeing and playing, between one passage and the next. And the body by itself can also learn, e.g., to adapt itself to changes of climate.

Purposiveness? But the elaborately purposive organization of growth and life is mostly unconscious.

Intelligence ? Where then is the sharp line that we must draw between the instincts of the body and the intelligence of the mind ? If we define intelligence so stringently as to set it clearly apart from instinct, its manifestations in any one personality will be so rare that we must suppose Mind to be dozing through most of our active life. But such a sharp separation mangles the facts. In reality, instinct and intelligence spring from one root, are inextrícably intertwined, and cannot plausibly be referred to different "substances." The most gifted imaginative writers, and not a few scientists and philosophers too, confess that their highest flights of genius are not solely the fruit of conscious deliberation, but owe much to patterns of ideas which seem to come into consciousness from outside, and to flow under their own momentum.

The materialist concludes that the real source both of our impulses and of the movements by which we respond to them is to be found in physical states. It is the mechanical movement of our bodies which determines both feeling and action. And when, as often happens, a man is subject to a conflict of motives, he will not be betrayed into talking of the war between " flesh " and " spirit," but will bear in mind that contrary physical tendencies exist in the body itself which may produce this sense of conflict and strain in experience.

33.—MATERIALISM AND HUMAN DIGNITY

To most of us this conclusion is bound to be somewhat unwelcome. It is both an affront to our pride and a blow to our hopes to tell us that our actions are the effects of nothing more unique or exalted than the revolutions of electrons, that what we shall do and think is inexorably fixed by physical conditions, and that the integrity of our personalities is entirely dependent on the integrity of our brains. Some people, who are not much concerned with the hope of a future life, thinking this one a sufficient trial, may find compensation for their injured dignity in the even greater injuries to the dignity of pretentious persons who profess to know all about the nature of the soul and the entrée to a prosperous future life. They may feel it a relief to be assured that there is nothing in the world more mysterious or powerful than the familiar everyday Matter. They may find it heartening to think that our welfare is in our own hands, to be achieved by a careful study of that nature which is within range of our observations, and a bold striving to win mastery over her. But to most of us the materialist conclusions are daunting and disappointing. We would rather have felt ourselves more highly privileged members of the cosmic society ; we would rather have felt that there were other powers in the universe more like ourselves and more sympathetic to our aims, instead of having to leave to blind material impulses the last word in everything.

But we must take care not to exaggerate the difference which the acceptance of materialism makes to our estimate of our situation in the universe. Nothing in human life is made any the less valuable by being assigned to a material cause. From the way in which the word " materialistic " is often used as a vague term of moral abuse, one might suppose that a materialist philosophy must make men less appreciative of the " spiritual values." But there is no necessary connection between philosophical materialism and low tastes, or indeed any particular kind of tastes. Aesthetic beauty and nobility of character are what they are, and are worth admiring and appreciating, whatever be the causes from which they arise.

34.—DETERMINISM AND FATALISM

Again, we are apt to suppose that Materialism makes every individual the helpless sport and prey of external material forces, and this induces in us a feeling of constraint, of frustration, of ultimate helplessness in the face of unfeeling dominating powers. In this feeling there is some illusion. We must be careful not to confuse the Determinism of materialist philosophy with Fatalism. Fatalism is, strictly, the doctrine that the ultimate outcome of any series of events is determined in advance, and that whatever we do about it we are powerless to prevent it taking place. Human decisions are able to affect the details of their fortune, but not its essentials. This view is really inseparable from the idea of an intelligent designer, Fate or God or the Gods, who has decided and planned the general scheme of things. Oedipus was condemned by fate to kill his father ; and so, even though he was exposed in infancy on the hillside, some controlling force intervened to bring him to a meeting with his father and engineered the quarrel which led to his father's death. I know of no evidence for this theory, and find it hard to see what evidence there could be.

The determinist, on the other hand, holds indeed that the future is fixed, in the sense that there is only one possible future having regard to all the present circumstances. But he does not hold that the future is fixed despite all that we can do. On the contrary, every action of every human being must make some difference, and may make a great deal of difference, to the fortunes of himself and other people. So Determinism is not, like Fatalism, a counsel of despair. It does not say, " What is the good of trying ? ", but insists that my trying always makes a difference to the result. Certainly, there are some things beyond my powers, physical, mental, and moral, and it is no good attempting them. But these limitations are facts which every theory must recognise.

Nor is the picture of a human being in the grip of remorseless alien forces altogether a correct one. Certainly, the materialist tries to discover what makes me desire and choose what I do desire and choose in particular situations. But the desires are nevertheless *my* desires, and the choices *my* choices, and no philosophical theory can alter the fact that I sometimes achieve what I desire. It is misleading to contrast myself with the forces within me which determine my will. They *are* myself, they constitute me ; and within limits I can modify them by voluntary action.

The notion of constraint or compulsion applies properly to my relation with other bodies or personalities, things outside me and different from me. I am compelled when some other physical object pushes or pulls me, or some other person by dire threats induces me to do what I do not want to do. But in the arising of a desire there is no such constraint ; there can be none until desire has arisen ; for constraint only exists in its opposition to desire.

The mistake is encouraged by the way in which some people talk of *laws of nature.* For this inclines us to think that a scientific law is the same kind of thing as a human law. A human law is a command backed by threats, a means of compulsion on the persons subject to it, and whoever is subject to a law is liable to constraint. But the laws of nature are not imposed by anybody on anybody else. They are not commands, and there are no penalties for breaking them. They are simply the ways in which things (and people) actually behave. To say that a person acts according to law is simply to say that he acts according to his character. Thus materialism does not make men unfree in the most usual sense of the word. It does, however, make human character and desires derivative, the result of other influences which are neither human nor even living. And this is, no doubt, a blow to our self-esteem. But wounded pride is no argument against a theory, though it is often enough a motive for rejecting it.

Such is the materialist philosophy. We cannot pass judgment on it until we have considered the alternatives, but a provisional assessment of the evidence for it is called for here.

35.—CONCLUSIONS: ALL MENTAL PROCESS IS ALSO PHYSICAL

It seems to me that there is good ground for accepting at any rate one part of the materialist case : viz., that there are no mental processes which are altogether separate from and independent of the body, but all mental processes are associated with corresponding physical processes and cannot be carried on without them. Nothing happens in the world without the expenditure of physical energy, the displacement of matter or radiation in space; and this applies to changes in human consciousness as well as to everything else. This thesis is far from being proved. We can by no means prove that there is any special difference between the brain of a man who is thinking about cricket, and the brain of a man who is thinking about the Peloponnesian War. But it seems to me a good deal more likely than not, on the available evidence, that this is the case. The further we carry our researches, the more confirmation we receive of the principle that there is no consciousness without its material background.

36.—WHAT ABOUT TELEPATHY?

The most serious difficulty for this principle is probably that presented by the occurrence of telepathy; that is, the communication of the content of consciousness—thoughts or images or sensations—from the mind of one person to the mind of another without the use of speech, visual signs, or any sensory means of communication. There is an abundance of evidence that this kind of thing sometimes happens. There is no known or imaginable physical agency by which telepathic communication could be effected, and no physical explanation of it which has any degree of plausibility. But I do not think it wise to put much stress on this ignorance of ours. Our knowledge of telepathy and its conditions is very slight and rudimentary. And if we can think of no explanation of it along physical lines, we can think of none along psychological lines either. The facts are not likely to be explained by reference to physical processes and laws at present known. But it seems to me rash to conclude that telepathy takes place without any modification of the state of the brains of the persons involved.

37.—AND SPIRITUALISM?

There are, indeed, persons calling themselves " spiritualists " who allege that they have good evidence of the existence of disembodied spirits, viz., the souls of deceased persons. But their claim is weak. A great deal of this evidence is neither more nor less than deliberate fraud. More of it is the result of unintentional self-deception. What remains, and will bear rigorous scientific investigation, is very small in amount, and very equivocal in nature. It comes mainly through mediumistic communications, mixed up with a good deal of what is obviously unreliable fantasy. And it is susceptible of many explanations. That which refers to the existence of disembodied souls of the deceased is only one possible explanation, and that a very vague one. For the supposed communications from the dead have not given us any very clear or coherent account of the nature of their disembodied existence or of the manner in which they communicate with the living. Some " spirits " have indeed told us things which living persons in normal states of mind and enjoying normal powers could not know or guess. But a medium professing to communicate with the dead is not in a normal state of mind ; and we have the alternative of explaining the communications by reference to abnormal powers of embodied minds ; for these there is independent evidence. I am far from denying outright that human personalities can survive the bodies with which they are associated. But I am denying that spiritualism and psychical research have yet produced adequate reasons for thinking that they do. If they do survive and can communicate, it is very extraordinary that, out of the countless millions of surviving souls, only a few dozen have so far taken the trouble to do so.

38.—CONSCIOUS PROCESSES DO HAVE PHYSICAL EFFECT

One part of the materialist thesis, then, seems to m
probably true. Another part, however, seems to me probabl
false. This is the doctrine that consciousness makes n
difference to the material processes which it accompanie
To carry out this doctrine in all seriousness, we have t
maintain that I, as a conscious mind, never *do* anythin
whatever, but only become aware of what my body is doing
my decision to type this page and my reflection on the meanin
of its contents have nothing at all to do with making the word
appear on the paper. The causes of this happening ar
brain-changes which, though usually accompanied b
consciousness, produce their effects by a physical influence t
which consciousness is irrelevant, and might just as well no
be there. Likewise, we must suppose, my own experience
make no difference to other experiences of mine. When
carry out a train of reasoning—" My wife's coat is on th
hall-stand, and in this weather she would never have gon
out without it, so she is still in the house "—my awareness o
the premises of my inference has no influence on my comin
to believe the conclusion, which is produced by physica
causes quite independent of awareness.

If, then, we are to take this doctrine quite seriously, w
must suppose that I am subject to an incessant illusion, th
illusion of actually doing things. I, and as far as I can mak
out other people too, have the feeling that we are agents a
well as patients and observers in the world ; we feel that w
can decide, and that our deciding makes a difference ; bu
for that feeling the materialist philosophy can provide neithe
justification nor explanation. We have the feeling that som
of our conclusions are determined by the consideration o
their premises ; and on the materialist theory, that is a
parallel illusion.

The rejection of such elementary features in our experienc
of living seems to me to demand pretty strong proof befor
we can submit to it. Such a strong proof we cannot obtain

We shall not obtain it until we can produce a thorough and detailed account of all the activities of mind in purely physico-chemical terms, deducible from the laws of physics and chemistry alone ; and that we are very far indeed from doing.

There is, after all, a great difference between the behaviour of a conscious and of an unconscious man ; and the plausible assumption, in line with the prompting of inner experience, is that consciousness makes a difference. If we really believed in Epiphenomenalism, if we really seriously held that the activity of man was nothing but a physical process, which might equally well be performed by a creature without consciousness, it is hard to see what good ground we should have for believing that other people were conscious, and not merely unconscious automata.

But the clarification of this matter requires a more careful investigation of what exactly a physical process is, what are our sources of information about the nature of physical processes, and when we are entitled to call one process the " cause " of another. This will be better done when we have considered the challenge to the whole basis of the materialist case which is put forward by the rival school of Idealism.

FURTHER READING.

Systematic statements of thorough-going materialism are hard to find. E. Haeckel—*Riddle of the Universe*, is a famous one. A modern example is J. J. C. Smart—*Philosophy and Scientific Realism*. For the physical facts, C. G. Darwin—*New Conception of Matter*, or R. E. Peierls—*The Laws of Nature*. For the philosophical interpretation of modern physics, L. S. Stebbing—*Philosophy and the Physicists*.

The main facts about the brain and nervous system are given in most text-books of psychology, e.g., R. S. Woodworth—*Psychology*, chap. 8. See also C. S. Sherrington—*The Brain and it Mechanism*. W. McDougall—*Body and Mind* discusses this problem.

For telepathy and " spiritualistic " phenomena, G. N. M. Tyrrell—*Science and Psychical Phenomena ;* C. D. Broad—*Lectures on Psychical Research.*

V

BERKELEY'S CRITICISM OF MATERIALISM

39.—WHAT IDEALISM IS

"IDEALISM" in the broadest sense of the term can cover any kind of philosophy which maintains that the fundamental reality is Mind or Spirit, and that Matter either is not wholly real at all, or at any rate is a subordinate and dependent reality. In this sense Idealism has been common enough in the philosophical thought of all ages, and has been the dominant type of philosophy in India at all periods, and in Europe throughout the Dark and Middle Ages. In a narrower sense of the word, Idealism is a modern type of philosophy, which has been developed since the establishment of the experimental sciences, and has been formed in sharp and conscious opposition to Materialism. Modern Idealism is essentially the philosophy which denies that Matter, as conceived by the physicists and the materialist philosophers, is an independent reality, or indeed a reality at all in the full sense of the word. It is the aim of the idealists to undermine Materialism by showing that its supposed ultimate reality is in fact a creature or a dependant of Mind.

40.—IDEALISM AND COMMON SENSE

This doctrine is at first glance a paradox, an affront to common sense as well as to science and scientific philosophy. And idealists are conventionally supposed to be visionary, fanciful thinkers, with their heads in the clouds, out of touch with the firm facts of life. The non-philosophical sense of " idealist," meaning a man who confuses his ideas with the facts, has abetted this notion.

The most persuasive defence of idealism against this complaint is to be found in the writings of Bishop Berkeley (early eighteenth century), which have had much influence on the development of modern idealism. He claims that, however paradoxical it may look at first sight, idealism—the doctrine that matter is unreal—is actually nearer to common sense than is Materialism ; and he also claims that his idealist philosophy sticks more closely to the given facts of experience, that it is the materialists who go beyond these given facts to build fanciful pictures based on their own thoughts instead of on observations.

Berkeley's first claim cannot be upheld : idealism does come into collision with common-sense ideas about the world, as will be shown hereafter. But I do not think this is a matter of great importance. Common sense is no infallible guide to philosophical truth. There would, indeed, not be much point in the study of philosophy if common sense had already discovered for itself the answers to the problems we are investigating. That there exist witches and fairies, that the earth is flat and the sun goes round it, that women are incapable of higher education, that it is dangerous to sleep with the bedroom window open, have all been firmly established principles of common sense in their day. And as for more strictly philosophical matters, it is a gross error (though one which philosophers often commit) to suppose that " common sense " has a single consistent view about any question seriously in dispute among philosophers ; it is for the most part in hopeless confusion about them. You can easily test this by putting a few philosophical questions to a few unphilosophical acquaintances. We are apt to take it for granted that what seems obvious to our own " common sense " also seems obvious to that of other people ; but if they have been brought up in a different intellectual atmosphere, this may not be so. Nevertheless, there are certain assumptions about the nature of the world which are so confidently believed by so many people that we should be reluctant to come into collision with them, and should scrutinise with the greatest care any argument claiming to overthrow them ; and the belief in an independent material world is one of these.

Berkeley's second claim is, I think, sound. Whatever other idealists may have done, he, at least, has tried to make philosophy live within its income, to keep as close as possible to the facts of experience, and to admit nothing as real unless it can be found to be real by actual observation.

41 —HOW DO WE KNOW THAT THERE ARE MATERIAL THINGS?
THE COMMON-SENSE ANSWER

But is not the reality of material things a matter of direct and immediate observation ? Let us examine this claim. First, taking the standpoint of the unphilosophical and unscientific person, let us inquire what sort of thing a material object is. This table on which I am typing will do. Common sense assigns to it such characteristics as these : it has a length and breadth and height (3-ft. x 3-ft. x 2½-ft.) ; it has a colour (a particular shade of brown) ; it is hard and firm and solid ; and these characteristics it has constantly retained for some twenty years. It has a stable position in space (2-ft. from the wall, 5-ft. from the door). It exists there outside me, independently of me, and continues to exist whether or not I am looking at it or touching it or thinking of it, and whether or not anybody else is doing so. It can be observed by other people besides myself, and is in fact being observed now by my wife at the other side of the room. Permanence, independence, publicity, are all essential attributes of the table. There is only one such table in the room, and it has been here continuously (apart from a few temporary absences at spring-cleaning) for many years. Other material objects have different shapes, sizes, positions, colours, etc. ; but they all, as material objects, share these characteristics of permanence, independence, and publicity. All this the ordinary person will say without hesitation.

If the philosopher now asks him " How do you know that there is such a thing as a table ? ", and he is willing to humour his interrogator so far as to answer this obviously idiotic question, he will reply " Because I can see it and touch it." The philosopher continues " Then the table is that coloured shape which you see when you open your eyes, that hard firm expanse which you feel when you stretch out your hand ? " The plain man says " Yes " ; and, so saying, is straightway involved in contradictions from which there is no escape without some modification of what he has already said.

42.—ITS DIFFICULTIES

For, let us consider. The table-top is said to be square. But, as I look in front of me at what is alleged to be the table, I see something which is not square; the end nearer to me is wider than the end further from me . . . The table is smaller than the door, and larger than my hand. But, if I compare the objects in my field of vision, I find that " my hand " takes up more space than " the table," and " the table " takes up more space than " the door " . . . The table is approximately of the same colour all over. But, as I now look at it, in the uneven light from the window, with the shadows cast on it by typewriter and books, it shows a dozen distinguishable shades of brown, white, and black ; and as the day advances, these patches of colour change their positions on the visible surface . . . If I now get up and move round the room, I see a series of different shapes, different sizes, different colours . . . If I press my eyeball with my finger, I can see two objects where before I saw one. Which of them is the table ? And what on earth is the one which isn't the table ? For I assume that there is still only one table there.

43.—SENSE-DATA

We can go on like this indefinitely. There are plenty of ways of showing that the qualities assigned to the material

thing, the table, are not identical with the qualities of the coloured shape which I see. The two are not the same thing.

This coloured shape has no name in ordinary language. We speak of " seeing the table double," but have no ordinary word for each of the two shapes which are then seen. Descartes, Locke, Berkeley, and their contemporaries, called these direct objects of sense-awareness " ideas." This is an unfortunate term, for it causes confusion with other senses of the word " idea." Normally, to " have an idea " of a thing means to think about it as contrasted with looking at it or touching it ; on Berkeley's usage, to " have an idea " of a thing very often means to look at it or touch it. Modern philosophers have coined the word " sense-datum " as an unambiguous technical term to distinguish the visible object from the material object. In the same way, we have to distinguish sense-data of hearing, touch, etc., from material objects. I shall generally use this term, and I shall say that from the above argument it is clear that the sense-datum and the material thing are not identical. In the sense of the word " see " in which I can see coloured shapes, so as to be directly aware what shape and colour they have, I cannot see the table, and I do not know of its existence by seeing it. Since common sense persists in saying that I see tables and other material objects, the word " see " must have more than one meaning. Philosophers have decided to use the verb " to sense " in place of the ambiguous " see," " feel," etc., to stand for my awareness of sense-data.

44.—THE SCIENTIFIC ANSWER

This point, however much it may disturb the plain man, is neither disturbing nor novel to the scientist and the materialist philosopher. Both physics and materialist philosophy require the distinction which has just been drawn between sense-data and material objects, between things as they appear and things as they really are. For if physics tells us the truth about the world, then material things must be a good deal different from the appearances presented to the senses. The sense-datum of the table is a continuous expanse which remains still ; the material table as described by the physicists consists of an enormous number of tiny particles sparsely scattered in space, all in continual rapid motion. The materialist philosophy must insist that our senses do not show us material reality.

Materialism also offers us an account of the relation between these two entities. This relation is causal. Physics and physiology between them explain the causal process in some detail. In the case of sight, rays of light strike the table and rebound to strike the retina of the eye. A stimulation of the optic nerves is carried to the brain, whereupon, we must suppose, a sense-datum comes into existence, whose qualities vary according to the nature of the stimulus. The area of the retina affected, and so the shape, size, and position in my visual field of the sense-datum, depend upon the shape, size, and position in physical space of the material table. The colour of the sense-datum depends upon the wavelengths of the light reflected from the table. Thus the table is not *the* cause of the occurrence of the sense-datum. Its causes are complex, and its immediate cause is a state of the brain and not of the table. But, in the causal process which gives rise to the sense-datum, the material object has a key position. For the qualities of the sense-datum are determined by those of the corresponding material thing. The differences between the sense-data I obtain when I am looking at a table, and those I obtain when I am looking at a pig, are due to the differences between the material table and the material pig.

But, while the materialist abandons the common-sense account of the nature of the table in many respects, yet in certain fundamental respects he accepts it and uses it in his explanations. The material table is no longer brown, or hard, or smooth, if these words are taken as descriptive of sense-qualities. But it still has a definite size and shape and position, not identical with but closely related to the size,

shape and position of the corresponding sense-data. And it still has those essential characteristics which I emphasised in speaking of the Plain Man's Table ; independence (it exists whether or not it is being observed) ; permanence (it persists as the same thing over a considerable period of time) ; and publicity (sense-data caused by it can be sensed by many different observers).

45.—ITS DIFFICULTIES

We must now put to the physicist or to the materialist philosopher the question we recently put to the plain man, and ask " How do you know that this material table of yours really exists, and how do you know what are its properties ? " This question seems as ridiculous to him as it did to the plain man. For both of them begin their systematic thinking by taking the existence of physical things for granted, and neither of them thinks of questioning this belief except under philosophical criticism. And the natural response of the physicist is the same as that of the plain man : " I know that material things exist because I can see them and touch them."

But from this answer his own theory debars him. For on that theory the material table is not what I see, hear or touch ; I see, hear and touch only visual, auditory and tactual sense-data. Yet there is not much doubt that when the physicist began his investigations he took for granted that his senses told him the truth about the material world ; and in interpreting his observations, he still constantly assumes that in certain essential respects the properties of his sense-data are also properties of material things. He concludes from his researches that there is a difference between them ; but this conclusion is reached by assuming that *some* material things at least are as he sees and feels them to be—for instance, the readings on his balance or thermometer. He can tell us how he came to disbelieve that material things really have colours and smells ; but he cannot tell us how he came to believe that material things exist ; like everyone else, he has believed that for longer than he can remember, and never questioned it. This, however, does not really matter. Our question to the physicist or the materialist philosopher is " In the light of your present knowledge, what good reasons can be given for the belief that material things exist, having the properties which you assign to them ? "

46.—LOCKE'S REPRESENTATIVE THEORY OF PERCEPTION

In the later seventeenth century, when the physicists' account of the process of sensation was still something of a novelty, the English philosopher John Locke tried to answer this question, and his solution has been very commonly accepted by materialist philosophers. It runs along these lines. We do not immediately perceive material things, but only sense-data, which Locke calls " ideas." It is conceivable that we might confine our attention to the sensing of sense-data, and not become aware that there are material objects at all. But in practice, we cannot rest in the mere sensing of sense-data, but must go on to try to understand what they are and where they come from. As soon as a man reflects upon the nature of his sense-data, he must realise that they have causes which lie outside himself. These causes are what we call material things. There are, indeed, some experiences of mine, those of imagining and remembering, of which I am myself the cause (or at least part-cause), so that I need not refer to an external world to account for them. But imagination and memory are clearly distinguishable from sensation. Locke says " If I turn my eyes at noon towards the sun, I cannot avoid the ideas which the light or sun then produces in me. So that there is a manifest difference between the ideas laid up in my memory, and those which force themselves upon me, and I cannot avoid having. And therefore it must needs be some exterior cause, and the brisk acting of some objects without me, whose efficacy I cannot resist, that produces those ideas in my mind, whether I will or no.

Besides, there is nobody who doth not perceive the difference in himself between contemplating the sun as he hath the idea of it in his memory, and actually looking upon it."*

So, on Locke's theory, the material thing, while not directly known as an object of sensation, is indirectly known as the cause of my sensations. The assumption that there is a material world is necessary to account for the fact that my sensations occur at all. Furthermore, it must be a material world of a particular kind. The assumption that there exists a material table 3-ft. square, 2½-ft. high, 5-ft. from the door, etc., together with the laws of optics, explains how I come to have the particular sense-data that I do have when I say that I see the table.

Thus sense-data, while not material objects themselves, are the means by which we reach a knowledge of material objects, and it is mainly for that reason, and not for their own sakes, that we are interested in them. They represent material things to us, and we can take their qualities as indications of the qualities of their causes. Hence this type of theory is called the " representative " theory of perception. It has also been expressed by saying that sense-data " mirror " the external world.

They do not represent or mirror it exactly. On the contrary, as we have seen, there are a good many discrepancies between the sense-datum and the material thing which it represents. Nevertheless, in certain fundamental respects there is a correspondence between them. According to Locke, it is only in the " primary " qualities of things (shape, size, position, motion,) that sense-data resemble their originals. " The ideas of primary qualities of bodies are resemblances of them, and their patterns do really exist in the bodies themselves ; but the ideas produced in us by secondary qualities have no resemblance of them at all. The particular bulk, number, figure and motion of the parts of fire or snow are really in them whether anyone's senses perceive them or no. But light, heat, whiteness or coldness are no more really

Essay on Human Understanding, Bk. IV, chap. XI.

in them than sickness and pain." *   Thus, if my table appears in my visual field between the chair and the wall, I can safely refer that same spatial relation to the three corresponding material objects.   In the case of the secondary qualities, I cannot say that the brownness which I sense belongs to the material table, but I can infer that there is some other quality in the material table which causes it to appear brown rather than any other colour.   So Locke's answer to the question which began this discussion is that we know that there are material things because we know that our sense-data have causes outside ourselves ;   and we know what they are like because in certain respects sense-data resemble them.

47.—CRITICISMS OF LOCKE'S THEORY

The representative theory of perception has for long periods proved satisfactory to the working scientist.   But the objections brought against it by Berkeley and by subsequent thinkers are so formidable that few philosophers of the present day are satisfied with it.   Let us look at these objections.

(1)   No adequate reason is given for putting primary and secondary qualities on an entirely different footing, and saying that shape and motion in the sense-datum resemble shape and motion in the material thing, whereas colour and sound do not.   All the arguments which can be brought against supposing that the qualities of the sense-datum are identical with those of the material thing apply equally to primary and secondary qualities.   If the colour of the sense-datum varies according to the position of the observer, so does the shape of it.   The sense-datum caused by a straight stick half-immersed in water is not straight but bent ;   and most of us have experienced the illusion of movement when our train was being passed by another train in a station.   If, therefore, the possession of colour by a sense-datum is not a good reason for attributing colour to the material thing which is its cause, the possession of shape by a sense-datum is not a

Essay, Bk. II, chap. VIII, secs. 15 and 17.

good reason for attributing shape to the material thing either—
I do not mean that particular shape, but any shape at all.

(2)   Even if there *is* a resemblance between sense-datum
and physical object, we could never find out that this was so.
In order to find out whether A resembles B, we must examine
A and examine B and compare the results ; or, if we cannot
directly inspect them, we must have indirect information about
the properties of each of them independently.   But this,
according to the representative theory, is precisely what we
are never able to do.   We can examine the sense-data ; but
we cannot examine the material things, for according to this
theory it is only sense-data, and never material things, that
can be directly observed. ⁻ Nor have we any other source of
information about the character of material things except
sense-data.   How can we know that A resembles B if we
can examine A but not B, and if all our beliefs about the
nature of B are derived from its supposed resemblance to A ?
This has usually been reckoned the most convincing argument
against the representative theory.

(3)   Berkeley argues in this way.   Supposing that there
did exist, outside my experience, things resembling my
sense-data, what sort of things would they be ?   They would
be colour-patterns, sounds, etc. ;   that is, they would be
sense-data (or, as Berkeley calls them, " ideas ").   Redness,
for instance, is a sensory quality, and anything that was red
would be a visual sense-datum.   But sense-data, with all their
properties, are essentially mental, existing only " in the
mind," in the process of being sensed   Their being is to be
perceived, and they " have no existence without the mind."
" There was a sound, that is, it was heard."   To assert the
existence of any such entity, apart from the apprehension of
it by some mind, is absurd and self-contradictory.

If, therefore, there are other entities resembling my
sense-data, they must be other sense-data sensed by other
minds.   " An idea can be like nothing but an idea."   A
sound which nobody heard would not be a sound at all, and
the very supposition of an unheard sound is an absurdity.

Thus, if by " material substance " we mean something that has some of the properties of sense-data, but is not itself a sense-datum, then the notion of material substance is self-contradictory.

On this point, materialists wish to draw a distinction between colour, sound, etc., and shape, motion, etc. But this distinction is unfounded. Roundness is just as much a sensory quality as redness is. (Or rather, it is two sensory qualities, one a mode of seeing, and the other a mode of touching. For visual roundness and tactual roundness are two different properties, and it is only by experience that we come to associate looking round with feeling round.)

Shape and motion are, then, qualities of sensations, and, if they belong to anything else, it can only be to other sensations. Indeed, they are quite inseparable from the secondary qualities ; shape is the boundary of a colour-patch. We can see or imagine a visual shape belonging to a particular colour-patch, or a tactual shape belonging to a particular touch-sensation, but we cannot see or imagine a thing which has shape, but neither colour, nor hardness—or—softness, nor any other secondary quality. So the whole notion of a material thing contradicts itself. When we think of material things we are in fact thinking of our own sense-data, and projecting them, not only outside our own experience, but outside all experience whatsoever. This projection cannot be justified ; for a sense-datum cannot exist without someone to sense it.

(4) The doctrine of Matter is offered as an explanation of the occurrence of sense-experiences. But in what way does it explain these experiences ? Here before us is our sense-world of coloured shapes ; the existence of this world is supposed to be made more intelligible by assuming that there is outside it another world of colourless shapes of which our coloured shapes are inaccurate reproductions. But how impulses from that material world get themselves transformed into the contents of this different sensory world, nobody has claimed to be able to conceive.

We think, indeed, that we know what we are talking about when we speak of material processes. We think we can imagine well enough what sort of thing the real table is which is partly revealed to us and partly hidden from us by the sensory table ; but this is an illusion. For what we imagine is *ideas :* the imagined table is just as much a subjective, private creature of the mind as the sense-datum. In fact, material substance is not imaginable, for we can imagine only the sort of thing we can observe, namely, sense-data. The representative theory of perception places material things irrevocably beyond all possible observations, and encloses each of us in the circle of his own sensations and images. To postulate beyond that circle an unobservable, unimaginable, and therefore unintelligible world of Matter can hardly help our understanding ; it can explain nothing.

The force of this objection is concealed from us because we see that scientists are constantly describing their material world in terms which seem to us quite ' familiar and intelligible. But when we look more closely at these descriptions, we find that they are really descriptions of sense-data ; the scientists tell you what they see and hear, or what they might have seen and heard ; or else they tell you nothing you can make head or tail of.

It comes to this : either the material world is just a reduplication, a ghostly double, of the world of sense, in which case it adds nothing to what we have already got, and can do nothing for us which our sense-data cannot do more effectively ; or it is a different world, related to our sensations as cause to effect, in which case we have absolutely no means of getting at it and discovering its properties. It is only our sense-data we can observe and understand.

VI

PHENOMENALISM

48.—THE NON-EXISTENCE OF MATTER

FROM such arguments as these, Berkeley draws the conclusion that Matter does not exist, or at least there is no good reason for believing that it does. This seems a most alarming conclusion. But he assures us that there is no cause for alarm, if we are careful to understand exactly what he is saying. He is denying that there is any such thing as material substance as the materialist philosophers define it ; that is, a substance apart from and independent of all awareness, permanent, public, the cause of our sensations, having shape, size, position, motion. He is not denying that there are such things as tables and chairs and clouds and apples and cats, or that we know quite a lot about them and often make true statements concerning them. It is true that there is a table in this room, that it is 3 feet long, etc. It is true that grass is green and snow is white. It is true that water is a compound of oxygen and hydrogen, and malaria is caused by the bite of a mosquito. These statements are false if they are interpreted as referring to some unobservable " material " thing which is outside all experience. But there is another way of interpreting them in which they may well be true. That is to take them as descriptions, not of a mysterious unexperienceable Matter, but of sense-experiences which people have or might have.

49.—THE MEANING OF WORDS

And this seems a reasonable way of interpreting our statements when we consider how it is that we come to understand and make use of language. When I am teaching a

child the meaning of the word " table," I point to the table
so that he sees it ; I put his hand to it, so that he feels it
that is, I cause him to sense certain sense-data. Surely it
with these sense-data that he thereupon associates the soun
" table " ; when he sees and feels similar sense-data, h
repeats " table." It is by the differences in what they loo
like and feel like that he distinguishes tables from chairs an
apples and half-crowns. It is natural to conclude that whe
he uses the word " table " or " apple," he is using it t
describe what he sees, feels, tastes, etc., rather than t
propound some theory about an invisible and intangibl
material substance.

The word " table " *means* a certain visible squarene
and brownness, a certain tangible hardness ; i.e., it mear
a certain type of sense-experience. When I say " There is
table in this room " I am describing the sense-data which
am now sensing, and if I do not sense such sense-data, ther
being a truthful person, I do not say that there is a table i
the room. If someone else says that there is, I test his state
ment by looking and feeling, i.e., by finding out whether th
appropriate sense-data are available ; if they are not,
dismiss his statement as false. If I say " Socrates drank h
companions under the table," I am not describing an
sense-experiences which I have now, but I am describin
sense-experiences which I suppose Socrates and his companion
to have had at another time and place.

We cannot, of course, identify " the table " with any on
single sense-datum ; an experience which was entirely uniqu
and did not recur would not be worth naming. The functio
of words is not to name everything we see or hear, but t
pick out the recurrent patterns in our experience. The
identify our present sense-data as being of the same group o
type as others which we have sensed before. A word, the
describes, not a single experience, but a group or type o
experiences ; the word " table " describes all the variou
sense-data which we normally refer to as appearances o
sensations " of" the table. So a material thing is not indee

lentical with any sense-datum ; but neither is it something
ifferent in kind from sense-data. It is a group, or class, or
ystem of sense-data ; and nothing but sense-data goes to
onstitute it. So this doctrine may be expressed by saying
hat every statement we make about a material thing is
quivalent to another statement about sense-data.

50.—PHENOMENALISM

This analysis of the notion of a material thing is called
henomenalism, since it makes of a material thing a group
f phenomena, appearances, instead of a transcendent reality
istinct from appearances. It is a widespread view, and has
een accepted by many philosophers who do not call
hemselves Idealists and are far from accepting Berkeley's
iew that the fundamental reality is Mind. The term
idealism " itself, however, though it has shifted in meaning
nce, does properly denote just this part of Berkeley's theory,
hat the material world—" the whole choir of heaven and
rniture of the earth " says Berkeley—consists of what he
lls " ideas " and I have been calling " sense-data." The
ord in this sense has nothing to do with ideals, and the
heory would have been called " ideaism " but for con-
derations of pronunciation.

Phenomenalism, then, is the doctrine that all statements
bout material objects can be completely analysed into
atements about sense-data. The analysis of any such
atement must be very complex ; and the value of the
material-object language " is that it enables us to refer in
ne word, such as " table," to a vast number of sense-data
iffering very much among themselves. The group of sense-
ata constituting the table includes all the different views I
n obtain at different distances, from different angles, in
ifferent lights, no two of them exactly alike, but all of them
ariations on one central pattern ; it includes sense-data of
uch, and those of sound (though these last seem somewhat

more loosely connected with the main visuo-tactual group)
and with other kinds of material things, such as apples
sense-data of taste and smell form important constituents of
the thing.

51.—ITS ADVANTAGES

This type of theory has certain clear advantages. On
the representative theory, the very existence of a material
world or of any given material object must always be in
principle doubtful. I am directly aware of my sense-data
and so can be certain of their existence and character : but
" material objects " are quite different—their existence and
character can be known only by an inference, which cannot
give the complete certainty which comes from observation.
Descartes, for example, accepts this consequence of the
theory, and will not allow himself to believe that there is a
material world at all, until he has convinced himself that there
exists an omnipotent and benevolent God who would never
have led him to believe in the material world if it had not been
real. But if Descartes really succeeded in keeping up this
attitude of doubt for more than a moment, few men have been
able to imitate him. We *cannot* believe that the existence of the
table is in any way subject to doubt.

The phenomenalist theory, by making the existence of
the table *the same thing* as the occurrence of certain sense-data
removes that doubt ; for the system of sense-data constituting
the table has beyond doubt come under my observation.

The theory not only removes the doubt, but makes it
clear why we cannot seriously entertain it. The Plain Man
was right after all : material things are seen and touched
are objects of direct awareness, and it is by seeing and
touching that we know that they exist, though no material
thing is straightforwardly identical with what I am seeing and
touching *at this particular moment*.

So, by accepting the phenomenalist analysis, we escape
being involved in any reference to an unobservable Matter

We can preserve our empiricism inviolate, and talk about the things we see and hear and smell and touch, and not about other hypothetical things beyond the reach of our observation. Science, the knowledge of nature, on this view becomes the recording, ordering and forecasting of human experiences. Therein lies its interest for us. If the physical world lay outside our experience, why should we be concerned with it ?

52.—CRITICISMS OF PHENOMENALISM

But these advantages of phenomenalism are purchased at a cost. Along several different lines the phenomenalist interpretation of our statements about material things seems to conflict with our usual beliefs, and produces paradoxes not very easy to accept.

" APPEARANCE AND REALITY "

(1) In ordinary speech we are accustomed to draw a distinction between " appearance " and " reality," and to allow that a thing may appear to be what it is not, as Descartes' stick half under water may appear bent although it is really straight. Hence we reckon some of our perceptions as " real " or " true " or " genuine," and others as " illusions." The representative theory of perception is in accordance with this way of thinking ; for on that theory our sense-data are in some respects copies of material things ; some are accurate copies, and so are genuine and true, others are inaccurate copies, and so false and illusory. The representative theory differs from common sense mainly in holding that the discrepancies between the sense-datum and the material object which it represents are greater than we realise.

But what is the phenomenalist to make of this distinction ? He can admit no essential difference between appearance and reality ; for on his view the appearances *are* the reality. Material things consist of appearances—sense-data—and of nothing else. And these sense-data all actually occur and so are equally real. Moreover, they are what they appear to be ; their reality consists in appearing, and the suggestion that they might " really " have qualities which they do not appear to have is without meaning. Thus the phenomenalist has no justification for classifying them into " real " and " unreal ", or " genuine " and " counterfeit." The various sense-data which go to constitute a material object, such as my table, are of many different shapes and colours. All of them are equally real, and none of them can be *the* " real shape " or " real colour " of the table. Evidently tables are more versatile objects than we thought, and may have as many different shapes and colours as there are occasions of observing them. Why then should we come by the idea that there is only one " real shape," and the rest are mere appearances ?

The phenomenalist solution of this difficulty is to allow that in a strict philosophical sense of the word " real," the distinction between reality and appearance cannot be drawn. But the purpose of the common-sense distinction between appearance and reality is not to pry into the ultimacies of metaphysics, but to enable us to deal with the experiences we encounter. What causes us to condemn an experience as an " illusion " is that it leads us astray. A mirage is an illusion because it causes us to make a mistake. But what kind of mistake ? Surely, not the mistake of thinking that we now see trees and water, but the mistake of expecting that we shall soon be able to have a drink and sit in the shade. The mistake consists in the false expectation of certain other sense-data. Thus the illusoriness is not in the sense-datum itself, but in the expectation which we form when we sense it.

Error of this sort is possible because sense-data are not chaotic, but in the main are arranged in orderly series. Normally, when the visual sense-data belonging to water are obtainable, so are the gustatory sense-data of drinking water and relieving one's thirst. The mirage deceives us because, abnormally, we get the visual sense-data without the gustatory ones. Mirror-images may deceive us because the things seen in a mirror cannot be observed from the back and cannot be touched. Thus a " real " table consists of a complete set of sense-data of different senses related to one another in certain systematic ways (e.g., visual sense-data become continuously smaller and auditory ones continuously fainter as we move away from a certain region of space). When, as in the case of a table seen in a mirror, you have some members of the set but not others, you say that what is seen in the mirror is not a " real " table, or is not " really " there.

Again, the stick in water may lead us into error because sticks that " look bent " usually " feel bent " as well ; and so we are surprised to find that it " feels straight," and say that though it " looks bent " it is not " really bent."

The precise interpretation of the word " real " is different in different contexts. But in general, say phenomenalists, it will be found that what we call the " real world " is not a world different from that of appearances ; it is a selection from the world of appearances, a collection of appearances which are normal, systematic, and so reliable. The " unreal " consists of eccentric appearances which in one way or another fail to fit in with the normal type of sets of sense-data, and therefore cause us to form false expectations.

53.——THE PERMANENCE OF MATERIAL THINGS

(2) Sensations come and go. Few of them last for very long, and none of them lasts for ever. If we add up all the occasions in my life on which I have been looking at this table, we get a very short period indeed. And, like the rest of my species, I frequently go to sleep, and cease to perceive any material object whatsoever. That is to say, if a material thing consists of sense-data, its existence must be intermittent. Sense-data belonging to the thing exist only now and again, and most of the time they do not exist at all. But material objects such as tables are normally supposed to be permanent things, which endure uninterruptedly for very long periods.

How can a permanent object be made out of momentary sense-data ?

If I am alone in the room and close my eyes, there are then no sense-data belonging to the table ; are we to suppose that I can annihilate so substantial a material object simply by shutting my eyes ? It seems as though the phenomenalist must deny that any such statement as " There is a table in the room " can be true unless there is someone there seeing or touching it ; and he must also deny that any such statement as " The table has been here for twenty years " can be true, unless (what seems most improbable) gangs of watchers have been observing it in relays for the whole of that time.

54.—PHENOMENALIST ANALYSIS OF PERMANENCE

The phenomenalist answer to these difficulties involves a radical reinterpretation of the whole notion of a permanent material thing. That the existence of the table should be permanent in the way in which my waking experience is uninterrupted, that the table should last for twenty years in the way that my hearing a performance of a symphony can last for three-quarters of an hour, is of course impossible on a phenomenalist view. Whatever kind of permanence is attributed to the table must be understood in another sense.

Clearly, when I say that there is a table in the now uninhabited attic, I am not describing the sense-data of anyone. But, though the statement cannot be a description of *actual* sense-data, it can be a description of *possible* sense-data ; and this is what it is according to phenomenalists. To say that there is a table there now is to say that *if* there were anyone in the room he *would be* having the kind of experience which we call seeing a table. " There is a table " means " Go and look and you will see a table." And to say that it has been there twenty years means that if at any time during those years anyone had been in the room, he could have seen or touched a table.

So we must modify our original account of the nature of a material thing. It consists not merely of actual sense-data, but also of possible sense-data ; or, more precisely, of the fact that under certain conditions sense-data are obtainable. What is permanent is then not any sense-datum or group of sense-data, but the possibility of obtaining sense-data of a certain kind. Hence J. S. Mill defined matter as " the permanent possibility of sensation."

I think this much at least must be admitted : if it is true that there is a table in the attic, it is also true that if anyone with the use of normal eyes in a good light were to be in the attic now, he would have the experience of seeing the table ; if it is true that the table has been there for twenty years, it is also true that if anyone has been there under those conditions at any time during those twenty years, he would have had the experience of seeing the table. That is to say, the statement about sense-data is involved in or implied by the statement about the table. According to the pheno-menalist, such statements about possible sense-data constitute the whole of what the statement about the table means. All statements about material objects are equivalent to statements about what people have experienced, or would have experienced if circumstances had been different.

He points out that if we try to imagine the presence of the table in the attic, what we do is to imagine what it would look like and feel like. If we want to test the statement that it is there, we go and look. Statements which are not, in the final analysis, about actual or possible experiences, cannot be tested at all, and are therefore without meaning for us.

55.—BERKELEY'S ACCOUNT OF PERMANENCE

Berkeley himself gives another explanation of the permanence of material things. According to his theory, God is eternally perceiving everything, and therefore, at times when neither I nor any other human being or animal is perceiving the table, God is still perceiving it. But whether or not this is really the case, it is obviously not a correct interpretation of what we mean when we attribute continuous existence in time to the table. For if it were, we should not believe in permanent material things at all unless we believed, not only in God, but in an omnisentient God such as Berkeley believed in.

56.—CAUSAL ACTIVITY

(3) According to our ordinary notions of them, material objects are causally active : they do things. The table supports the tablecloth, the fire warms the room. Material objects exercise force, have influences on one another and incidentally on ourselves, causing, among other things, our sensations of them. This continually active causal interplay makes up the system of nature, which it is the business of science to study and reduce to laws. Does not science explain what happens by referring events to their causes, which in the material realm at least are material things, exercising physical force ? Surely, the room cannot be warmed by my visual sense-datum of a fire ! Still less can it be warmed by the possibility of a visual sense-datum of a fire during my absence, when I am not looking at the fire but the room gets warmed all the same. When we all sit round the table and sense sense-data very similar in shape, size and colour, what is the explanation of this fact, if not that there is an independent table which is the common cause of all our similar sense-data ? Berkeley himself admits, or rather insists, that an " idea " is " inert," and can *do* nothing.

57.—PHENOMENALIST ANALYSIS OF CAUSATION

To deal with this problem, we need a fresh analysis and re-interpretation of the notion of cause, parallel to the phenomenalist re-interpretation of the notion of " substance " or " thing." Such an analysis was given in David Hume's *Treatise of Human Nature* (1739), and modern phenomenalists in the main follow his line of thought. Hume's aim is to interpret statements about cause and effect in such a way that the relation between a cause and its effect shall be an observable fact, and shall contain nothing mysterious or occult. For unless the words " cause and effect " described something we could observe, they would not, according to Hume, be intelligible to us.

What, then, do I observe in cases in which I should naturally use causal language ? I am watching a game of billiards. I observe the event which I might naturally describe by saying that one ball A moved across the table and made or caused another ball B to roll into a pocket. What do I actually *see* ? I see a certain sequence of events : first the movement of A, then the touching of A and B, then the movement of B. This temporal sequence of movements, the one which I call the effect following on the one I call the cause, seems to be all the visible relation there is between them.

But obviously, mere temporal sequence is not the same thing as causation ; *post hoc* is not the same as *propter hoc ;* plenty of other things preceded the movement of my billiard-ball in time which were not causes of it. Yet nothing seems to be observable but temporal sequence—first one event, then the other. Whence do I get this notion of the ball being made or caused or forced to move ?

If I were pushing the ball myself, I should be aware of myself making a certain muscular effort, *trying* to make it move ; and, when I observe the collision of the two balls and the ensuing movement of B, I may perhaps have a vague image of a similar kind of pushing going on between the balls. But if I do, it is clear that this feeling of muscular effort is not observed in the situation presented to my senses, but is a " projection " of my own past feelings in similar situations. For billiard balls do not have muscles, or make efforts, and even if they did, I could not observe what efforts they were making, I could only observe their movements.

Certainly when I see the collision, I expect that the second ball will move—there is a " felt tendency of the mind " to pass from the " cause " to the " effect " ; but this is a psychological fact about me, not a physical fact about the balls. There seems nothing in the observed situation corresponding to the words " cause," " power," " force," which I am inclined to apply to it ; only the observed sequence of one event on the other. But how, then, do I distinguish between those temporal antecedents of an event which are its causes, and those which are not ? How do I establish the difference between *post hoc* and *propter hoc* ?

The answer is plain enough ; I repeat the experiment, and if the same sequence of events recurs, I conclude that it was a causal and not an accidental sequence. The reason I believe that the movement of the ball was caused by the impact of the other ball, and not by somebody lighting a cigarette at the same time, is that I know by long experience that balls always move when they are struck by other balls moving fairly quickly, whereas they do not usually move when men light cigarettes in their neighbourhood. When medical men inquire into the cause of cancer, what they are looking for is something which always happens to a man before he becomes ill with cancer, just as, when they say that malaria is caused by the bite of a mosquito, they mean that a man has always been bitten by a mosquito before developing malaria. The observable fact which leads us to say that C is the cause of E is the fact that events of the kind C are followed by events of the kind E, not once or sometimes, but whenever they occur.

Causality, as a fact about the world, is then, according to Hume, a relation of invariable sequence. What is required to convert *post hoc* into *propter hoc* is regular repetition. To say that every event has a cause is to say that for any event E there is another event (or complex of " conditions ") C such that whenever an event of the kind C occurs, an event of the kind E follows. It is to say that the sequence of phenomena is patterned, systematic ; that there are in nature discoverable regularities.

But these regularities are discoverable among the observed phenomena themselves, and not between phenomena and something transcending phenomena. Causation, thus interpreted, is a relation between sense-data. The causes, that is to say, the invariable antecedents, of sense-experiences, are other sense-experiences.

Of course, not all causes are actually observed phenomena. In the analysis of cause, as in the analysis of substance, we must sometimes refer to possible sense-data which are not actual. But to say, for example, that a burst pipe was caused by the formation of a lump of ice which I have not seen, is not to desert the realm of sense-data ; it is only to refer to sense-data which were not actually observed, but which might, in principle, have been observed ; if I had been in a position to look at the interior of the pipe, I should have seen a lump of ice there.

Thus Hume and his followers do not deny that the relation of cause and effect is a real feature of the world ; but they interpret it as a relation between sense-data, actual or possible. So the principle of causality does not carry us beyond the sphere of the observed and the observable, or compel us to admit the existence of " material substance " over and above systems of sense-data.

Thus, on this theory, the material world consists of sets of sense-experiences, together with the fact that an indefinitely large number of other similar sense-experiences might be had under certain specified conditions. Its " substances " are orderly groups of sense-data ; and its causal relations are relations of regular sequence between sense-data of specified kinds. The main business of science is to discover causal laws, i.e., to reveal the patterns in that complex of experiences we call Nature. Science tells us what experiences to expect as the sequel to the experiences we are now having, and so renders our knowledge of the world systematic.

58.—KNOWLEDGE OF OTHER MINDS

(4) But this solution of the problems of substance and causality brings to light a further grave difficulty for Phenomenalism. This is the problem of our knowledge of

other minds. Among the objects which make up the world about me, I include conscious experiences of other people which I suppose to be similar to my own. Among the items of my knowledge and reasonable belief about the world I include such facts as : that Smith is annoyed, that Jones has a stomach-ache, that Brown is hopeful, that my cat wants to be fed ; all of which appear to be facts about conscious experiences other than my own. What is the nature and source of my knowledge that these other minds exist, and of what is taking place in them ?

It is evident that my knowledge of other people's experiences is not direct. Telepathy is no exception to this ; for, though it seems that there are telepathic experiences whose source is in the minds of other people, the percipient is not as a rule aware of this fact and does not recognise the experiences as belonging to someone else's consciousness. It is possible that there is an element of direct non-sensory awareness akin to telepathy, in our ordinary intercourse with other people, but if this is so, it is evidently in the highest degree vague, meagre, and unreliable. If it is not quite the whole truth, it is at any rate very nearly the whole truth, that all our knowledge of other people's minds comes through sense-perception, through observing their bodies and the effects of their actions.

My reason for believing that Jones is a distinct constituent of the world about me is that I can observe a distinct group of sense-data—visible features, audible tones of voice, etc.— having the same kind of relation to one another as those of any other material thing. My reason for believing that Jones is an entity independent of myself is that I have no control over the behaviour of this group of sense-data—e.g., I hear him utter words which I had not intended to say. My reason for believing that Jones is a mental being is that his behaviour is of the sort which in my own case is the expression of conscious purpose—e.g., his talk sometimes makes sense, he puts food into his mouth as though to nourish himself, etc. My reason for believing that Jones is a persistent being is in part an analogy with my own persistent consciousness through time, in part that I find evidence of the effects of his activity over periods of time when I have not been watching him—e.g., I find letters signed " A. Jones " and dated yesterday, or I leave him in the room with a glass of whisky and return to find him smacking his lips over an empty glass. That is to say, the mind of Jones is something whose existence I do not observe, but infer as the unobserved enduring cause of my intermittent sensations ; and my belief in the persistence and causal activity of his mind is intimately associated with my belief in the persistence and the causal activity of his body, for the acts of talking, eating, etc., whereby he manifests his mentality to me are physical acts.

Now this sort of argument for the existence of other minds is essentially the same as the argument given by Locke and other holders of the representative theory for the existence of matter ; and it is exposed to the same objections. The mind is an unobservable entity, postulated as the cause of observed phenomena. I have the same sort of reasons for believing that Jones continues to be conscious when he is out of my sight and hearing as for believing that the fire continues to burn when I am out of the room.

Logical consistency requires that the permanence and causal activity of Jones' mind should be interpreted in the same manner as the permanence and causal activity of the fire or of Jones' body. Thus a consistent phenomenalism must interpret the permanent existence of Jones in terms of the permanent possibility that I shall see him or hear him ; it must interpret the causal activity of Jones in terms of certain regular correlations by which changes in the sense-data constituting his body are connected with each other and with changes in other things. If it is impossible for me to conceive what I could not possibly observe, it is impossible for me to conceive your experiences, since it is impossible for me to observe them.

59.—OTHER MINDS; THE PHENOMENALIST THEORY

Many phenomenalists, determined to adhere consistently to their principles, have accepted this view of the matter. They have attempted to interpret statements about other people's minds in the same way as statements about other people's bodies, namely in terms of actual or possible sense-data occurring within their own experience. These sense-data will be what we should normally call perceptions of the body of the other person.

So, by a different route, phenomenalism arrives at the same behaviouristic interpretation of psychology as materialism did. The meaning of " Jones is angry " must be analysed into " Jones' fists clench, his eyes flash, his voice is shrill . . . ," i.e., the physical phenomena which on other theories would be said to be effects or symptoms of Jones' anger. " Jones is thinking about his girl-friend " is more difficult : it must be interpreted as an expectation that before long Jones will begin to talk about the girl, or assume a rapt and amorous expression, or, in the last resort, that if I ask him whether he is thinking about her, he will be heard to answer " Yes." Jones must become a system of sense-data, actual and possible, within my experience, just as the table is ; but the sense-data are related to one another in a more complex fashion than those of the table.

Once again, the phenomenalist may point in confirmation of his view to the way in which we learn the use of language. When I learn the use of the phrase " X is angry," it is not by inspecting the mental processes of X, but by noticing the physical " symptoms " which he displays ; in default of these physical symptoms, I should never learn that people got angry. (It is not very plausible to say that I first become aware of anger in myself, and come to believe in the anger of other people by analogical reasoning. A child is probably aware of the anger of its parents as something to be afraid of, long before he is capable of discovering the analogy between their anger and his own, which feels to him quite different.

Psychological terms apply in the first place to the moods of other people as expressed in their behaviour ; my own anger is not expressed by saying " I am angry," but by abusing the person I am angry with.)

60.—OTHER MINDS : BERKELEY'S THEORY

This interpretation of our statements about other minds is highly paradoxical. And it is not the explanation that Berkeley himself gives. He holds that, while the account of causation given in section 57 above is part of the truth of the matter, it is not the whole truth. The word " cause " refers to two quite different kinds of relation, of which one is a relation between phenomena only, but the other is not. In so far as causation is a relation between phenomena, the type of analysis given above is adequate. The causal laws of science are statements of regularities of sequence among observable events. But natural science does not exhaust the range of human knowledge. The regular sequence of phenomena is not the only type of causation with which I am acquainted. I am also aware of myself as a doer, a causal agent, who acts, makes efforts, and gets results.

Awareness of my own activity is, according to Berkeley, simplest and most obvious in thinking or imagining, where, by a mere effort of will, I cause certain " ideas " to be present to my consciousness ; e.g., I make up my mind to imagine a castle in Spain, and there it rises before my inner eye (though not, of course, in Spain). Here I am directly aware of an actual causal efficacy, aware both of the cause, my act of will, and of the effect, a change in my imagery. This is not a matter of regular sequence ; I do not need to try the experiment a great many times to make sure that I really did it. And it is not a relation between " ideas " at all, but between the activity of a " spirit " as cause and a change in my " ideas " as an effect. Much the same may be said of my voluntary physical activity, though here the situation is more complex. Where my own will is in action, there is true and genuine

causation, the work of a " spirit," and not of " ideas," whic
in themselves are " devoid of force or efficacy," and canno
be causes in the true sense of the term.

But it is quite clear that relatively little of what
experience originates in my act of will ; otherwise, I shoul
not have so many unwelcome experiences. I can choose wha
I shall imagine, I can choose in which direction to look, an
(within limits) to move, but I cannot choose what I shall se
or feel there. Consequently, Berkeley argues, I am not alon
in the world ; there must be other causes for the vast majorit
of the experiences I have. These causes cannot be the materia
substances of the scientists and materialist philosophers, fo
Berkeley claims to have shown that this doctrine of materia
substance is baseless and self-contradictory. But cause
there must be ; what are they ?

Only one actual efficient cause is known to me directly
namely, myself ; only one kind of causal activity, namely
the acts of will of a mind or spirit. Therefore, the onl
reasonable explanation of the experiences which I myself d
not cause is that they also are caused by acts of will of othe
minds or spirits. My sensations are produced by some othe
mind or minds, in the same way that I produce my ow
mental images.

No-one seriously doubts that this is true to some extent
there are in the world *some* other minds like mine, whos
activities affect my experience, namely, other human beings
and the behaviour of animals is sufficiently like my own fo
me to attribute to them a mentality of a kind. What of the
rest of nature ? There are no detailed resemblances between
the behaviour of the physical world in general and the
behaviour which is due to me or to other human minds ; but
the reasonable course, says Berkeley, is to attribute it to the
only kind of activity for which I have any evidence, that is,
the will of a spirit or spirits. He proceeds to assign the whole
of the process of nature, in so far as it is not due to other men
or animals, to a single spiritual agent, whom he calls God.

It is clear that it needs a great deal of reasoning to show that there is but one mind at work in the inorganic world and not several, and that this mind possesses the wisdom and goodness which Berkeley, in common with other Christians, wishes to attribute to God. These points are not adequately argued in his writings. He proceeds far too easily and lightly to the curious position that nature, in so far as its behaviour suggests intelligent purpose, is to be attributed to men, and in so far as it does not suggest intelligent purpose (at least on the surface), it is to be attributed to God.

But one may accept Berkeley's idealistic argument without making the precipitate leap to his theistic conclusions. One may say, with Leibniz, that the minds in nature are not one but an infinitely vast number, a separate mind, perhaps, to each material atom or electron (" monadism ") ; and then these other minds will be mostly low-grade and undeveloped as compared with ours. One may say, with W. K. Clifford and some moderns, that the substance of the world is, not fully formed minds, but a " mind-stuff," which is capable under certain conditions of developing into mind as we know it. One may say, with Hegel and an influential school which followed him, that the whole of reality *is* a single mind, whereof you and I are parts or aspects. But the consideration of such alternatives had better wait for a conclusion as to the validity of the general argument that the only real power in the world is spiritual power.

VII

PHENOMENALISM EXAMINED

WE thus have, arising out of this discussion, two questions to answer. (1) Is phenomenalism true, that is, can we take the series of sense-data as complete in itself and self-explanatory, or must we postulate some other kind of reality to be its source? (2) Is idealism true, that is, if we assume some other kind of reality to exist, ought we to assume that it is mental?

61.—THE RELATION BETWEEN SENSE-DATA AND MATERIAL THINGS

As to the first question, there is one point on which the argument seems to me quite conclusive. Our sense-data are not identical with physical objects, whether these are defined as the plain man, or as the physicist, or even as the phenomenalist defines them. They are not identical with the physical objects of the plain man or of the physicist, for both these persons require a physical object to remain unchanged in circumstances in which the sense-data certainly change. Both hold that the table does not change its shape when I change the position from which I look at it, whereas the sense-datum *is* changed. Unless these comparatively stable physical objects are assumed, the scientific explanation of sensation itself falls to pieces. As for the phenomenalist, even on his view no sense-datum is identical with a physical object, for the physical object is a system of possibilities, only a few of which can ever be actualised in any one experience. " This is a table " is never a mere record of what I am now observing, but involves the assertion that I and other people will be able to make further observations of a specific kind ;

and this possibility of further observations, which is part of what I mean when I say " This is a table," is not a matter of direct observation. So in any case our acquaintance with physical objects is not direct but mediate (to call it " inferential" would suggest a much more deliberate, self-consciously logical process than usually takes place). The properties of the sense-datum are not those of the material thing.

Yet—here is a paradox to be resolved—if I set out to describe a material thing, it seems that I invariably find myself describing sense-data. The table is square, brown, hard . . . all these, and all the other things I can say about the table, are expressed in terms of what is observed through the senses. Three alternatives are open to us here. (*a*) We can say that there is after all a real table which has some of the properties of our sense-data, though not all of them (Locke's theory). (*b*) We can say that the table consists of a set of actual and possible sense-data, which between them possess the properties which we commonly assign to " the table " (phenomenalism). (*c*) We can say that a statement like " The table is brown " is more complex than it looks. It must be understood to mean, not that anything in the world is both a table (a material object) and brown, but that there is some material object in existence such that, when it comes into a certain causal relation with a normal percipient under certain conditions, there will be a brown sense-datum in that percipient's experience.

Now for alternative (*a*) I cannot see any good reason. Once it is granted that we do not know the properties of the table directly, I cannot see any convincing reason for holding that it has any of the properties of the sense-datum. It cannot have them all ; any arguments which can be brought against its having one of them are equally valid against the others ; and we cannot produce any evidence of its having any of them except the observation of the sense-data themselves. We cannot, then, permit ourselves to assign to the material object any property of a sense-datum just because

it belongs to that sense-datum. We are not entitled, from
the square look of the sense-datum of the table, to infer
that the material object is square. We are left with the
other two alternatives.

62.—THE PARADOXES OF PHENOMENALISM

If we take the phenomenalist alternative, let us not do
so without being clearly and fully aware of what it involves.
(1) It involves the denial that physical objects are permanent,
or exist unperceived. It must be granted to the phenomenalists that when I say " There is a table upstairs," I
am at least implying that if you were to go upstairs and look
(given normal eyesight, normal lighting, etc.) you would have
certain visual sense-data. But it seems quite clear to me that
this is not the whole nor the essential part of what I am
asserting. For when I say that the table is there, I am stating
something about what exists or happens *in fact, now ;* my
statement is about the actual present, and not, as the
phenomenalists make it, about the possible future. And if the
phenomenalist account is to be accepted, we must say that
this statement is a mistake. There is nothing at all in the
attic now ; there is no attic now at all ; for there is nobody
perceiving it.

(2) We must very seriously revise our opinions about
the nature of causality. As a rule, we are in the habit of
believing that a cause is something which actually exists or
occurs, and that something which does not actually exist or
occur can have no effects. This opinion must be given up
if we accept the phenomenalist view. For on that view, to
say that the bursting of pipes is caused by the formation of ice
in them is to say that whenever one observes or could observe
sense-data of the set constituting a burst pipe, one either has
or could have previously observed sense-data of the set
constituting a lump of ice inside that pipe. But quite clearly,
in practically every instance of this rule, nobody does actually
observe the ice ; the sense-data of the ice are possible, not

actual. That is to say, causality in such a case is a relation between something and nothing, between an actually observed burst, and a hypothetical proposition to the effect that if something had happened which did not happen and in practice could not have happened, then something else would have happened which also did not happen. This interpretation flouts our usual assumption that what might have happened but did not happen can have no effects. The actual material agents of physics and common sense must be replaced by a set of hypothetical facts relating to unfulfilled conditions. If this is so, it is difficult to see why we should suppose that these hypothetical propositions are true. If I leave a fire in my room, I expect it to be warm on my return ; but is this not because I believe that the fire is still now burning, a real present fire exercising an influence on a real present atmosphere ? I cannot see what reason can be given for expecting the room to be warmed, independently of my reasons for supposing that the fire *is* burning *now* (and not that, *if* I went and looked, I should see flame). I can see reason for believing in regularities in nature holding between one event and another ; but no reason at all for believing in regularities holding between one event which happened and another which might have happened but did not.

(3) A similar paradox arises with regard to other persons. According to the phenomenalist theory, all the statements I make about the consciousnesses of other people must be interpreted in terms of actual or possible observations of my own. A statement like " Jones is bored but he is not giving any sign of it " is a contradiction in terms, for on this theory the boredom *is* the signs. The only experiences I can intelligibly talk about or think about are my own, and whatever is not expressible in terms of actual or possible observations of mine is not intelligible to me. That is, there is no good argument for phenomenalism which is not an equally good argument for solipsism—the doctrine that the only experience in the world is my experience, and the only person existing in the universe is myself.

These paradoxical conclusions have been accepted by able philosophers, and one cannot therefore say that they are beyond belief. But they are markedly at variance with the ordinary assumptions, not only of common sense, but also of scientific investigation (for, whatever some scientists may manage to persuade themselves, they are not concerned only with the cataloguing and ordering of phenomena, but believe themselves to be dealing with permanent and independent objects). Hence we must demand very strong reasons indeed for accepting them.

63.—SOURCE OF THE PARADOXES : THE NATURE OF SENSE-EXPERIENCE

I think that those who accept the phenomenalist analysis do so mainly for one reason. They believe that the only alternative to it is an analysis which employs some " transcendental " terms—that is, terms which claim to refer to entities wholly different from anything ever met with in the experience of the persons who use those terms. Phenomenalists hold that no transcendental term can be intelligible ; and I think that they are right. But I do not think that this commits us to phenomenalism.

It does so only if we accept a particular account of experience which phenomenalists usually assume, but which seems to me seriously defective, since it overlooks elements which are genuine factors in everyday experience. Its mistakes arise in large part from taking up, in the investigation of experience, a theoretical, contemplative attitude, and forgetting that this, which is the normal and proper attitude of the philosopher, is not either the normal or the proper attitude of ordinary people at ordinary times, including of course the philosopher himself when he is off duty. The result is that a description of the experience of the introspective psychologist, engaged in the analysis of his own mind for the purpose of understanding theoretical matters, is mistakenly passed off as a description of the experience of all men at all times. From this theoretical standpoint, sense-data are like pictures in galleries, objects which we inspect or examine for their own sakes, which we take as detached, self-contained realities, to be analysed and fitted together into patterns.

But this standpoint is abnormal. The usual prevailing tone of our experience is that of action and passion, of commerce with an environment. Sensation is a phase in that commerce, and its function is to convey to us the activity of the environment, and to stimulate us to the appropriate responses. Hume, when he is talking of sense-data, uses the tell-tale word "impressions"; and I think that in many ways "impressions" is a better word to use than "data"; for, generally speaking, the experience that I have of sensations is not that they are given or presented to me, but that they are thrust upon me. No feature of Berkeley's account of experience is so surprising as his untroubled assurance that sense-data—"ideas"—are "one and all *inert*." Could there be a more extraordinary description of a loud bang or a flash of light? With visual sensations this account has some plausibility, though even there it is false; with sensations of other kinds it has very little plausibility.

I shall, therefore, say that, whatever Berkeley's or Hume's experience may have been like, the experience from which my own knowledge of the world arises is not an awareness of sense-data, taken as complete, self-contained existences. It is an awareness of an environment which acts upon me and upon which I react. And in it the function of sense-data is to make me aware of this ceaseless interaction; my awareness of sense-data carries with it an awareness that I am subject to the influence of other things, that my experience is being altered in this way and that by alien forces. I am interested in sense-data very little for themselves and their own qualities, and very much as indications of the nature of the things I have to deal with, and as clues suggesting the appropriate ways of dealing with them. The sense-datum is a cue for action. The sound of an explosion has in itself, as an auditory image, the qualities of volume, pitch and timbre.

But in primitive experience, before it has been subjected to psychological or epistemological analysis, its most outstanding quality is frighteningness—warning of something going on which I had better keep out of the way of.

The epistemological analysis, which separates out the sensory qualities of various kinds of sense-data, examining them in and for themselves, is an indispensable mental function. But it must not be allowed to obscure the fact that in ordinary experience these sensory qualities are not so detached, but are accompanied by an awareness of causal efficacy whereof they appear as the effects and the signs, an awareness of a directedness in the process of living, from other things to me in sensation, and back from me to other things in action.

"Consider," says Philonous in Berkeley's dialogues,* "supposing matter did not exist, whether it be not evident you might for all that be affected with the same ideas you now are." Hylas replies "I acknowledge it possible we might perceive all things just as we now do, though there was no matter in the world." Once this admission is made, there is no escape from solipsism. For the next step follows at once. It is then possible that Hylas might perceive the ideas of Philonous which he does perceive, though there was no Philonous in the world ; and he has already lost the right to say, as he does say, " *we* might perceive."

It is this possibility that sense-data might, for all we can perceive to the contrary, be complete independent realities, that I am challenging. For it seems to me that as given to us, as known by us, they are not so ; they are factors in a process of interaction between each person and other things in the world around him. The category of causality is then given, not as an order among sense-data, but as a relation between the self and those active things with which it is in contact. The growth of knowledge about the world does not consist in superadding an idea of the physical world to an original idea of myself and my experiences (here the phenomenalists are in

Dialogues between Hylas and Philonous, Dialogue II, near end.

the right), but is a sorting out into its various elements of that world which in its general nature is known from the start.

The same is true of the category of Space. My awareness of space does not seem to be simply an awareness of the fact that visual sense-data are side by side in a visual extension, and tactual sense-data spread out in a different way in a tactual extension, the notion of Space with a capital S being constructed by arranging these various sensory extensities in imaginary patterns. There are these detailed awarenesses, of course. But there is also, as it seems to me in my own experience, the more generalised awareness of an environing space, not as that *in* which sense-data are arranged, but as that *from* which influences come and *into* which I move out and pursue them. This space does not stop dead at the boundaries of what I can see or touch, but extends beyond— I want to know what is on the other side of the wall, and that tacit assumption that there is another side to it is as much a muscular urge to go and look as anything else. Anyway, it is a part of original experience.

64.—QUALITIES OF SENSE-DATA AND QUALITIES OF MATTER

So I shall assume that the initial awareness or " experience " from which my understanding of the world must set out is not an awareness of sense-data merely, but an awareness through sense-data of things in space. But it is an awareness of these environing things only as alien influences. It is not a revelation of their nature—still less of their " ultimate nature "—apart from their effects on me. For sensory properties do not, as far as I know, belong to the material thing in itself apart from its relation to me ; they belong to a process of sensing which arises out of the interaction between me and my environment. The nature of the sense-datum is due, it appears, partly to the character of the external stimulus and partly to the character of my reaction to it. In default of any information other than sense-data about the nature of external reality, I cannot be sure that any particular feature of sense-data faithfully reproduces the character of material things.   It is reasonable to suppose that sense-data vary with variations in the influences to which my experience is subjected, but not to suppose that they imitate the nature of those influences.   So the peacock's tail as we see it and the blackbird's song as we hear it cannot be said to exist in nature when we are not looking and listening.   Something surely exists, and peahen and blackbird presumably see and hear something like what we do ; but not just like it.

65.—WHAT DO WE KNOW ABOUT MATERIAL THINGS ?

What then are we entitled to say about the table as distinct from our sensations of it ?   Let us put it in this way. An experience is conceivable in which different impressions came and went at random, in which there were no steady, consistent recurrences of phenomena of the same type, in which therefore no order could be discovered.   Many dream-experiences are rather like that.   In such a world there would be no " things," and the distinction between " appearance " and " reality " would hardly arise.

But our normal experience is not like that ; it does contain regular and reliable patterns.   Whenever I turn my eyes to the middle of the room, I see that same brown squarish expanse ; whenever I reach out my hand before me, I feel that same hard smooth surface.   There is plenty of variation among my sense-data ; but there is also a certain kind of constancy (I will not embark on the laborious business of saying exactly what kind of constancy it is ; it is not quite the same for all kinds of material objects.)

Moreover, the table-sensations maintain certain constant relations to other ordered sets of sensations which also recur. The table regularly turns up above the carpet and below the ceiling.   This constancy of pattern marks off the table quite distinctly from the chair and the carpet and the rest.   In bringing out the character and the epistemological importance

of this " family " of related sense-data, the phenomenalists
have performed a valuable service to philosophy.

Now whatever in the world is the cause of this constancy
in my sense-data (and also in yours and other people's) is
what we call the material table. The character of the sense-
datum is dependent on many factors besides the table;
some of them, which are causes of variation, are called light,
eyesight, etc. The constant factor which is responsible for
the similarity in the series is called the table ; and its place in
space is the place at which the set of sense-data can be
obtained. Its persistent existence under observation is
evidenced by the continuous availability of visual and tactual
sense-data over periods of time. Its persistent existence
unobserved is evidenced by the persistence of other effects
which I have learned to associate with its visible presence
(e.g., it still supports the table-cloth and the typewriter when
I can no longer see it or feel it).

But what is here evidenced is a persistent factor in the
nature of things ; whether it is one single self-identical thing
lasting without appreciable change, as common-sense tends
over-hastily to assume, or a regular rhythm in a series of
vibrations in the ether, as some modern scientists have
suggested, or something different again, remains for further
consideration. And further consideration brings to light
that at least in some cases it is not one single property of
one single thing which determines the constant characters of
my experience. Brownness, for instance, which is one of these
constant characters, is found to depend upon a complex
relation between many different entities ; and what common
sense attributed without discrimination to " the table,"
science apportions among several different material things or
processes—the table in an exacter sense, the rays of light, the
sense-organs . . . My nose is much the same in appearance
as it was ten years ago ; but physiologists agree that there is
no one continuing entity, my nose, to which the same set of
properties has constantly belonged. On the contrary, my
present-day nose consists of different physical material from

my 1938 nose ; it is only the form which is the same. We must be prepared for the possibility that the table may in the same way be, not a single persistent thing, but rather a persistent form or pattern in events, as the light is. But whatever the persistent factors may be precisely, *something* persists.

The difference between this point of view and the phenomenalist's is not so big as it looks. For on either view it is only sense-data, actual or possible, which can be *described ;* and on both accounts it must be possible to *refer* to entities which are not actually observed (material objects, or possible sense-data). Indeed, the phenomenalist analysis of the meaning of our statements about material things seems to me in the main true, though I do not think it gives the whole meaning of those statements.

66.—THE DEFINITION OF MATTER

The upshot of Berkeley's criticism of the notion of material substance is, then, as follows. The doctrine that our sense-data have causes outside us to which we may give the label " matter " is not seriously shaken. But the doctrine that sense-data copy the qualities of matter is overthrown. And this makes an important difference to our understanding of Materialism.

Materialism derives some of its attractiveness from the apparently solid and vivid reality of material things. The table and rocks and water seem to be real inescapable facts of awareness ; they resist our efforts ; they bump us if we encounter them ; they are firm and indubitable. But the soul seems insubstantial, flimsy, intangible, and therefore dubious, so that we can throw doubt on its reality without flying in the face of facts. This is a mistake. The hardness and firmness of the table, even its continuous solidity, are properties of our sensations, and these are not material objects—if the hard-and-fast alternative mind-or-body is to apply to them, it is not easy to say on which side of the frontier they will fall. There is quite a good sense in which, as Descartes insisted, the mind is better known than the body ; in that consciousness is an immediate datum, whereas the existence of a material object cannot be directly known.

So the effect of the phenomenalist analysis is to make the notion of a material object much less definite, less picturable, than it seems to be at the start. Briefly, if Matter means " That which is the cause of our sensations," or, more exactly, " those things or processes which determine certain systematic features of our sensations," if the material table is " whatever makes me see brown squarish shapes and feel hard smooth touch-sensations," then Matter certainly exists. But if Matter means a permanently existing object which either is a sense-datum or is just like one, then Matter does not exist. Only sense-data can be described and imagined ; Matter cannot. It follows that physical science, telling us of the characters of material substance, does not give us a description of the ultimate nature of reality. Indeed, it does not *describe* anything at all (except incidentally sense-data). Its conclusions are expressed in mathematical equations and formulæ which do not even appear to describe anything. What physics tells us is nothing at all about the *quality* of material reality, but a great deal about its structure and behaviour. It works out exact quantitative relations which hold between various kinds of changes going on in Nature, and it tells us what we may expect to observe as the sequel to previous observations in specified kinds of situations.

In the eighteenth and nineteenth centuries this view of the nature of physical science was a philosophers' rather than a scientists' view. Scientists tended to suppose more or less vaguely that the ultimate physical realities they had to deal with were like visual and tactual sense-data, like the hard, solid billiard-balls we can see and feel, only a good deal smaller. If they could not be directly perceived, they could at least be imagined.

But in the twentieth century physicists themselves have been compelled by the further development of their own science to abandon this view. It is now pretty well agreed among physicists that protons and electrons cannot be described at all in terms appropriate to the description of phenomena of the senses. In place of description, we have the equations of wave-mechanics, in which there is no attempt made even to assign a physical correlate to each term of the equation (some physicists say that terms in their equations correspond to " waves of probability "), but if we solve them we get results which apply to the measurements of certain laboratory phenomena. Thus the physicist Dirac says "The only object of theoretical physics is to calculate results that can be compared with experiment, and it is quite unnecessary that any satisfying description of the whole course of the phenomena should be given." The electron is something that behaves in such a way that physicists can make certain observations. Matter is " that which satisfies the equations of physics " (Bertrand Russell). We know of it that it does satisfy those equations ; and that is about all.

Thus, Materialism is not a complete philosophy. If it means that the laws of physics apply to everything in the universe, it may well be true. But if it means that physics gives an exhaustive account of the nature of anything, it must be false. Nothing can be entirely reduced to matter in motion. For nothing is *merely* matter—i.e., possesses only the formal properties of being in a certain place at a certain time and being the cause of certain changes of place in other things.

FURTHER READING.

Berkeley's theories are clearly expressed in *The Principles of Human Knowledge* and (a rather simpler version)—*Three Dialogues between Hylas and Philonous*.

For Locke's theory, see his *Essay on Human Understanding*, Bk. II, chaps. 1, 8, 23, Bk. IV, chap. 11.

For Hume's, see *Inquiry concerning Human Understanding*.

See also : H. H. Price—*Perception*.
B. Russell—*Problems of Philosophy*.
A. J. Ayer—*Foundations of Empirical Knowledge*.
R. J. Hirst—*The Problems of Perception*.

VIII

IDEALISM

I F, THEN, Matter is simply a system of diversified activities giving rise to various experiences, if physics gives us only a formulation of some of its structural properties or habits, the way is open for a further filling-in of the picture of nature. We can seriously consider the Idealist hypothesis that what is behind the curtain is the same as what is in front of it, that the diversified activities which give rise to our experiences are mental or spiritual activities analogous to our own ; that the world is after all a unity, but a spiritual unity, a great Mind or society of minds, whose thoughts, feelings, and volitions make themselves known to one another through the medium of sensation. What is to be said of this theory ?

67.—IS IDEALISM SELF-EVIDENTLY TRUE ?

The first thing to be said is that we must not be in too much of a hurry with it. The issue of Idealism cannot be settled by any simple and ready argument, either for or against. Berkeley thought that he could settle it in favour of Idealism with a short and simple argument which in essence runs : " The only agent in the world whose nature I directly know is myself ; and I am spiritual. Therefore all the other agents in the world are spiritual. The only kinds of things of which I have any knowledge are spirits and ideas. Since the causes of ideas are not themselves ideas, they must be spirits."*

This is a shockingly bad argument. Either it generalises for the whole universe from one single instance, or it tacitly assumes that there can be nothing in the universe except the

*See for instance *Principles of Human Knowledge*, para. 26.

kinds of things with which Berkeley was acquainted. And I can see no ground whatever for this bland and conceited assumption. Why should there not be active things in the world altogether different in character from ourselves ? It is true that, in so far as they are different from you and me, and from everything in our experience, we shall be unable to imagine them or to understand what they are like. But the impossibility of our adequately understanding them does not in the least prevent them from existing, and making a difference to our experience.

I think that those who suppose that nothing except experience can possibly exist, have slipped into this false principle from the true principle that nothing except experience can be imagined or described. Thus F. H. Bradley declares " Sentient experience, in short, is reality, and what is not this is not real," and gives as his reason " I can myself conceive of nothing else than the experienced." * But the world is not limited to what you and I and Bradley can imagine or describe ; and we may even have good inferential grounds for believing in the existence of things whose nature we cannot know. There are few more persistent sources of error in philosophy than the arrogant presumption that what the philosopher cannot know cannot therefore be real.

68.—IS IT SELF-EVIDENTLY FALSE ?

But we must also beware of too hastily begging the question on the other side. Philosophers of many different persuasions have insisted so strongly on the utter and insuperable distinctness of Matter and Mind, that it seems paradoxical to suggest that the same thing might be both mental and material. Yet this sharp sundering of the two is by no means the work of common sense. In ordinary speech " you " and " me " and " Jones " are the names of personalities at once mental and bodily, having both such physical properties as

* *Appearance and Reality*, chap. XIV.

same identical effects—the system of nature—and both of them are known only through their effects.

There may, indeed, be a difference between our emotional attitude to a world described as the product of Matter, and to the same world described as the handiwork of God ; and in Spinoza's philosophy, it seems to me, the significance of the term God is almost entirely emotive ; Spinoza uses it because he wishes to express and suggest an attitude of reverence, and not because it gives any information about the nature of his Ultimate Reality. But surely an emotion which responds to the name instead of to the thing named is unworthy of a philosopher. What concrete difference does Idealism make to our vision of the world ? What is really at stake in the controversy between Idealists and Materialists ? Or is the whole argument a product of confusion of thought, as some modern philosophers have maintained ?

I think that this question admits, after all, of a simple and straightforward answer. A Mind or Soul or Spirit is an agent who acts with a purpose in view, whose actions are designed to achieve an end which seems to him worth achieving. The evidence for mentality in the universe must be evidence of the presence in it of design, of the adaptation of means to ends, of the pursuit of values. Let us now consider what this evidence amounts to.

70.—IS THERE A PURPOSE IN NATURE ?

On the face of it, it seems that some things in the world behave purposively, and others do not. The behaviour of men and animals can best be understood as the pursuit of a number of aims. I can tell whether a man will turn left or right at a crossroads if I know where he intends to go. I can tell what will stop my cat's mewing if I know whether he desires to be fed or to be let out or to be nursed. There is a good deal of resemblance between the aims of different men, and lesser resemblances between those of men and those of animals. My cat and I share a general interest in being fed, though there are some differences in detail in our tastes. To the extent that we have common interests, so far I can regard him with sympathetic understanding, and imagine what it is like to feel as he feels. And this interpretation of the experiences of other conscious beings by analogy with my own is the only way I have of attaining insight into the inner nature of things, as distinct from their effects on my senses. With animals the range of such understanding is narrow. With other men it is much wider, not only because there is a closer similarity between my mental life and theirs, but also because they are able by the use of language to give me information about their experiences and intentions which otherwise I should not know.

But in the behaviour of most of the objects about me, I find no evidence of activities analogous to my own conscious pursuit of aims. There is no parallel between what I do and what the table does. There is, indeed, a parallel between the behaviour of the table when it falls to the ground on being pushed over, and my behaviour when I fall to the ground on being pushed over—a parallel made precise in the quantitative laws of physics. But when I am pushed over, I am not *doing* anything at all. If I do anything in such a predicament, I do what tables cannot do, e.g., reach out a hand to steady myself. We cannot, of course, definitely prove that there is no state of consciousness which underlies and conditions the behaviour of tables or the falling of raindrops ; but we have no obvious ground for thinking that there is. For the behaviour of these things does not pursue any discoverable purpose, either their own or anybody else's.

The ancients sometimes tried to interpret the behaviour of inanimate things by means of the conception of the inner purpose of the thing—stones fell to the ground because that was their proper place ; sometimes by the conception of Fate, i.e., a purpose lying outside the thing itself—" every bullet has its billet." Neither of these conceptions helps us in understanding how inanimate things behave, and predicting what they will do next. Stones move in accordance with gravitational attraction, wherever it may take them, exactly as if they were simply passive, like a man falling over a cliff. Nor, in spite of soldierly superstition, do bullets decide whom they are going to hit and move around looking for him until they find him ; on the contrary, their course is determined entirely by the initial impetus imparted to them and the resistances they encounter on the way. Their behaviour is to be understood, not in terms of purpose, but in terms of uniform reaction to a given stimulus. One cannot conclusively prove that the bullet has no awareness of what it is doing. But it seems plain that if we were to credit the bullet with a mind of some sort, it would have to be a mind of a very rudimentary order, lacking the sensitiveness and discrimination which we possess, lacking anything worth calling thought or will, and capable only of fixed response to a very limited range of stimuli. The conclusion that it has a mind may, then, appeal to the metaphysician on grounds of theoretical tidiness ; but it can make little difference to the way we regard the world. We have not much basis for a sympathetic understanding of the mental life of bullets ; we have little enough for microbes.

So the serious issues of Idealism do not relate to the consciousness of bullets, nor yet to those of men, about which there is no dispute, but to consciousnesses of a higher order than men ; that is, to God, or the gods, or the Absolute Spirit. The question is whether the bullet fulfils, not purposes of its own, but those of a consciousness much more far-seeing and powerful than those of either bullets or men can be. The question is whether there is a general meaning of existence, a teleological explanation of reality at large, a genuine " scheme of things." If mind and purpose are dominant in the universe, it is not our minds and purposes that dominate.

The concept of a superhuman purpose is, roughly speaking, the concept of God ; and it is in this broad general sense that, for the time being, I shall use the term " God," and shall say that Idealism is essentially, in all its forms, a philosophy which believes in God. It is associated with the religious feelings towards the world, the attitudes of reverence, awe, trust, towards the supreme reality. Such attitudes are obviously inappropriate either to a world which is mainly inanimate, or to one consisting mainly of low-grade minds, but are appropriate to a world which contains, and is wholly or largely controlled by, a being or beings spiritual, but on a higher level of spirituality than ourselves.

IX

THE EXISTENCE OF GOD—THE COSMOLOGICAL ARGUMENT

71.—ARGUMENTS FOR THE EXISTENCE OF GOD

ARGUMENTS purporting to show that there is a God have been very numerous in the history of philosophy, and I can deal only with some of the most important. They may be placed in four groups : those arguing *a priori* from supposedly self-evident first principles ; those arguing from the general character of the system of nature ; those arguing from the particular character of the religious and moral experiences of men ; and those arguing from the alleged miraculous powers of historical personages. Arguments of this last type demand too much detailed literary and historical criticism to be considered in a book of this kind, and I shall not discuss them. My own judgment is that there is no really convincing evidence that any particular historical personage was God, or was the recipient of an exclusive revelation from God. Each of the other types of argument requires some discussion.

72.—THE ONTOLOGICAL ARGUMENT

Of the *a priori* arguments, some are of a type which can convince only those who already believe. In this class must be placed the so-called " ontological argument," which says : God is, by definition, a necessary being, whose essence involves existence ; to say that God does not exist is to say that a being which necessarily exists does not exist ; and this is a logical contradiction.

This argument depends upon a confusion of different meanings of " necessary." If God exists, it is presumably true that His existence is necessary, whereas that of other beings is contingent ; that is, God exists of His own power, and there are no conceivable circumstances by which He could be destroyed, whereas other beings depend for their existence on certain conditions, and their destruction is always conceivable. But this " necessity " is not logical necessity. If by a " necessary being " we mean one whose existence cannot be denied without self-contradiction, there is no necessary being. For there is never any contradiction between " God, if He existed, would have the characteristic X," and " God does not exist," whatever the characteristic X may be.

73.—ARGUMENT FROM THE INTELLIGIBILITY OF THE UNIVERSE

Again, people sometimes argue : " The Universe is intelligible ; therefore it must be the work of an Intelligence." This argument looks as though there were something in it so long as it stays on the level of pure abstraction. But when we ask what are the precise features of the world which make it intelligible, and distinguish it from other possible worlds which would be unintelligible, I think there is only one reasonable answer. The world is intelligible because there are *kinds* of things in it which behave in uniform ways, and so make it possible for us to generalise, and infer from one fact to another. In other words, Laws of Nature are discoverable. Does this show that the world has been intelligently planned ? I do not think it shows anything of the sort. There is no reason why one atom of hydrogen should not be made of the same stuff, and behave in the same manner, as another atom of hydrogen, in an unplanned world ; what ground could we have for supposing that they must differ ?

We may be misled here by the use of the word " law." A " law of the land " is a command imposed for a purpose.

But " laws of nature " are not commands. They are simply statements of the ways in which things regularly behave. When we talk of falling stones " obeying the law " of gravity, we do not mean that they would rather like to rise instead, but decide to fall on receiving their instructions.

74.—THE COSMOLOGICAL ARGUMENT

But there are, of course, more serious arguments than these. The most impressive among them are variants on a common theme ; they try to show that the existence of God must be supposed in order to explain how this changing world can have come into existence. It is said that Napoleon summed up the deficiencies of atheism by waving his hand towards the landscape and demanding " Who made all that ? " The most usual *a priori* " proof " of the existence of God elaborates this feeling that the world is not self-explanatory, but requires a more-than-worldly Supreme Cause who has made it and sustains it. There are many different ways of putting this argument. I will quote two of the most celebrated formulations of it from St. Thomas Aquinas, and then try to put the general argument in my own way.

75.—THE ARGUMENT AS STATED BY AQUINAS

St. Thomas says : " Whatever is in motion is moved by another ; and it is clear to the senses that something, the sun for instance, is in motion. Therefore it is set in motion by something else moving it. Now that which moves it is itself either moved or not. If it be not moved, then the point is proved that we must postulate an immovable mover ; and this we call God. If however it be moved, it is moved by another mover. Either, therefore, we must proceed to infinity, or we must come to an immovable mover. But it is not possible to proceed to infinity. Therefore it is necessary to postulate an immovable mover." This argument stresses a particular kind of change, movement ; but the same sort of reasoning will apply to other forms of change in this perpetually changing universe.

The impossibility of " proceeding to infinity " in the series of causal explanations is more fully argued in another of Aquinas' proofs, thus : " In all efficient causes following in order, the first is the cause of the intermediate cause, and the intermediate is the cause of the ultimate, whether the intermediate be one or several. Now if the cause be removed, that which it causes is removed. Therefore if we remove the first, the intermediate cannot be a cause. But if we go on to infinity in efficient causes, no cause will be first. Therefore all the others which are intermediate will be removed. Now this is clearly false. Therefore we must suppose the existence of a first efficient cause ; and this is God."*

76.—ANALYSIS OF THE ARGUMENT

The general principle of the argument is that the causal order of events investigated by the sciences is not self-sufficient, but requires a reference outside itself to show how it can continue to exist and to change ; it does not contain within itself any power adequate to account completely for what happens in it ; and therefore, to give such an account, we must look outside it to a cause freed from the limitations under which all causes known to us must operate.

Two principles are needed to make the argument effective. (1) Among the events with which we are familiar, nothing happens without a cause. But, more than this, no change takes place in the world without a cause outside the thing which changes. Nothing in the world is the complete cause of its own changes. Thus Aquinas assures us that nothing can move without being pulled or pushed by something else, i.e., no movable thing moves spontaneously. For in so far as a thing can change itself spontaneously, the scientist's search for causes of such changes is unnecessary.

(2) A series of causes and effects reaching back into the infinite past, in which each event in the series is the effect of

*Both quotations from *Summa contra Gentiles*, chap. XIII.

preceding events and the cause of subsequent events, is not
an acceptable explanation of the causation of any event.
Such an explanation is that offered by scientific theory.   It
may be quite correct as far as it goes ; but it does not give us
a *complete* explanation of the matter.   An explanation in
terms of preceding events which are themselves explained in
terms of other preceding events, and so on to infinity, is an
incomplete explanation, and one which on its own principles
can never become complete.   For it never gets to an ultimate
and sufficient cause.

Sometimes it is argued that the notion of an infinite
series of causes and effects, stretching backwards into the
past without any beginning, is self-contradictory ; for it
supposes that an infinite time has already elapsed, and this
is a contradiction.   But one may admit that such an infinite
series of causes is possible (as Aquinas does), and still argue
that it is no explanation, but requires a further explanation
to supplement it.   For, it may be argued, since every event in
the chain is dependent on its predecessors, it is not a complete
and final explanation of its successors.   Each event is
provisionally, but not completely, explained.   We still need
an explanation of why the series as a whole happens, what the
whole causal chain depends on.   There must, then, be an
ultimate source of change ; and a thing which changes only
in so far as it is affected by other things cannot be such a
source.   The ultimate source of change must be some being
not dependent on other beings, something which moves
without being moved, acts without being acted upon.   The
conception of this being whose nature is Pure Act, who
initiates change but is not himself changed, is the conception
of God.   For such a being is not to be found within Nature,
but must be supernatural.   Thus, if this argument is valid, a
universe cannot consist only of dependent or " contingent "
beings, beings which might or might not exist : it must
contain also an absolutely independent or " necessary "
being, on whom contingent things depend.

77.—CRITICISM OF THE ARGUMENT

This argument is not without force. It sets forth a point of view, a possible account of the nature of things which, if it is accepted, gives us a rounded and final explanation. And it brings to light some of the consequences, not all of them familiar, of accepting other schemes of explanation. But the argument does not do what it claims to do, that is, demonstrate conclusively the existence of God. It is not a " proof."

Clearly, the whole argument is cut off at the root if you deny the first assumption on which it rests, viz., that it is self-evident that all natural events have causes. Hume denied it, and many other philosophers have followed his lead. Is this denial unreasonable? Is there any logical absurdity in supposing that something might happen spontaneously, without being made to happen by some external agency? Like Hume, I cannot see that there is. The particular form of causal principle used by Aquinas, that nothing moves without being pulled or pushed by something else, does not seem to me even plausible. I think that plenty of things move spontaneously, and that I am one of them myself.

If, however, some such principle of universal causality seems self-evident to you, you will have to tread very carefully to make your premises consistent with your conclusion. Shall we say " Every event has a cause? " But then an act of God's will must also be caused by something else, and the conclusion of the argument, that there exists an uncaused cause, contradicts its starting-point. Is it, then, only some kinds of events which have causes? But if there are some uncaused causes in the world, there is no need to look outside the world for a supernatural cause. If there are none, how is it that we can be so certain that there must be uncaused causes, and at the same time be just as certain that none of the things or events we encounter can be one? The argument can be made to work only if we hold fast to the principle that every event has a cause when we are considering anything except an act of God's will, and drop it when we consider God's acts of will.

Again, one may deny the second assumption of the argument, viz., that an event cannot be fully explained by referring it to a series of precedent causes going back to infinity. In this case, too, it is not easy to produce a reason for denying the possibility of an infinite series of causes and effects which is not an equally good reason for denying the possibility of an eternally existing God. If it is possible that God has existed from eternity, it is equally possible that a perpetual sequence of natural events, each the effect of its predecessors, has existed from eternity. If, however, the series of events constituting the world must have had a beginning, then presumably the series of events constituting the existence of God must have had a beginning too. (Many theologians say that the existence of God does not contain any series of events ; His being is timeless. But I do not think that the words " timeless being " describe anything which we can imagine or conceive ; and hence the theory that God is a timeless being cannot provide an intelligible explanation of anything else.)

It may be allowed that an infinite series of natural events would contain no entirely independent member. Each cause would depend on some other cause. But why should it not be so ? If we can account for every event in the series, then we can account for the whole series.

78.—A " FIRST CAUSE " IS NOT GOD

Thus, the argument (commonly called since Kant the " cosmological argument ") is not logically conclusive, and its assumptions can be denied without absurdity. But even if it were conclusive, it would be very far from proving the existence of God. For (1) the argument shows, at best, that there must be at least one uncaused cause or unmoved mover. It cannot possibly show that there is only one. There are many different chains of causes and effects in the world. Why should they not lead back to many different uncaused causes ? As far as this argument goes, the universe might be crammed with unmoved movers.

Nor can the argument show that this uncaused cause must be met with outside the observable world of " Nature." It is true that there is not to be found in Nature, as far as we can discover, any being which is completely independent of other beings in all respects. But such complete independence is by no means required by the argument. If it proves anything, it proves that there must be spontaneous activity as well as derivative activity in the universe. But an agent may perfectly well act spontaneously in some respects and derivatively in others. It is a mistake to suppose that, because every member of a group is dependent on the other members, therefore the group as a whole must be dependent on something outside the group. And so we can readily admit that every object we encounter in the world is a " contingent " being, i.e., its nature is, at least in part, the result of the action of other things upon it. But at the same time we may hold that Nature as a whole, the sum-total of all these contingent beings, is a being self-sufficient, necessary, independent of everything else ; that is, the acts and experiences of each member of the system are dependent upon those of other members of the system, and not upon anything outside the system.

(2) In Aquinas' statement of the argument there is an enormous leap from the notion of the First Cause to the notion of God ; and for this leap there is no justification. There is nothing in the cosmological argument by itself to show that the First Cause, or any Uncaused Cause, must be mental or spiritual ; still less that it must be wise or good, or have any of the attributes of God as conceived by Christian or other worshippers. The association between this metaphysical postulate and the God or Gods whom men worship is forced ; they have in reality very little to do with one another. There

s nothing about a First Cause which might induce one to
worship it.

Thus the cosmological argument is effective enough
within the framework of a number of metaphysical
assumptions taken for granted by Aquinas and the philosophers of the tradition to which he belongs ; but without the
assumptions of this particular philosophical tradition it
cannot be an effective argument.   And the acceptance of
these assumptions, which are by no means self-evident, takes
one already a long way towards accepting the conclusions
which purport to be derived from them.   Those who are
already disposed to welcome the conclusion readily enough
accept the premises.   But those who are dubious about the
conclusion do not find the premises by any means certain.
The cosmological argument cannot convince the " Gentiles."

FURTHER READING.

The works of Aquinas are not easy reading.   F. C. Copleston—*Aquinas*
and E. Gilson—*St. Thomas* are helpful.   M. Pontifex—*The Existence of
God,* gives modern versions of the arguments.   See also R. Descartes—
Meditations.

X

THE EXISTENCE OF GOD: THE ARGUMENT FROM DESIGN

79.—THE ARGUMENT FROM DESIGN

I TURN now from the attempt to prove the existence of God from first principles, to consider whether we can derive from observation good evidence that our world is a planned world. Are there intelligent and intelligible purposes directing it which are wiser and more powerful than our own? Innumerable generations of worshippers answer with confidence that this is so; we have only to look around us to see everywhere the indications of a vast cosmic Design or Plan, which cannot have come into existence without a Planner. Even the representative of radical scepticism in the dialogue of the arch-sceptic Hume confesses in the end, after a searching criticism of the argument from design in nature. "A purpose, an intention, a design, strikes everywhere the most careless, the most stupid thinker; and no man can be so hardened in absurd systems as at all times to reject it . . . That the works of Nature bear a great analogy to the productions of art is evident, and according to all the rules of good reasoning we ought to infer that their causes have a proportional analogy." * Of all kinds of philosophical argument, this has been on the whole the most popular and the most effective in persuading the doubter that our human spirits are environed by other and vaster spiritual powers.

80.—EVIDENCE FROM THE STRUCTURE OF LIVING THINGS

The evidence is drawn, in the main, from the structure and behaviour of living organisms, animal and plant. Its main drift is accurately and succinctly stated by Aquinas

* *Dialogues on Natural Religion*, Pt. XII.

thus : " Some things are without understanding, yet they work for an end, because often or always they work in the same way to obtain the best end ; hence it is evident that they attain the end not by chance but by intention ; and since they must act towards the end not by their own but by someone's knowledge, they reach the end because they are directed by an intelligent being. There must therefore be such an intelligent being who directs all natural things to their end, and him we call God." *

The end or purpose towards which living things work is life itself, and for each species of living creature, life of a particular kind according to its habit and pattern. Life is, or involves, a peculiar and complicated balance of chemical factors, a balance intricate, always precarious, subject to constant and unceasing jeopardy from the actions of neighbouring things, living and not-living. To preserve it requires a constant, complex, varied, ever-changing activity of adjustment to the always changing opportunities, threats and problems which the environment presents. Every living thing possesses the means and the capacity to accomplish this continual adjustment which preserves the moving equilibrium of life. And each type of living thing does it in its own way.

If we examine the structure of a living thing, we find that, with exceptions so rare as to be negligible, every part of it contributes to the business of keeping alive, and efficiently performs some mechanical or chemical function useful to this end. The eyes see, the teeth chew, the fur keeps warm, the kidneys drain, the brain (if we are to believe the materialist) thinks. The bird's wing, the mammal's leg, the fish's fin, differ in just those ways which make the first adapted for flight, the second for running, and the third for swimming. Sometimes this adjustment is of an amazing intricacy and precision. The eighteenth century loved to compare the living organism to a watch, the finest example of mechanical ingenuity then known. But in the fitting together of many complex parts to achieve a result, not only the best watches,

*Summa Theologica, Part I, qu. II, art. 3.

but the finest products of twentieth-century technology, are crude and clumsy alongside the performances of " nature " in the same line. It is beyond doubt that living things are so constructed as to fulfil efficiently the purpose of living their special kind of life ; they are as if designed for a purpose.

Moreover, this design is evidently not that of the living creatures themselves. No living thing designs itself, nor is it designed by its parents, who have very little idea how it will turn out when they decide to procreate. It remains to postulate a designer other than and greater than the living creatures of the earth. And when we consider the uniformity which runs through all these designs, how wing and leg and fin, despite their differences, are all variations on a single pattern, it seems most reasonable to refer all this designing to a single Planner, who alone has sufficient control over the material to carry out his plans with the marvellous virtuosity which we observe.

Indeed, the mind of the organism, so far from being the designer, seems to be itself part of the design. The bird's beak and wings would be of little use to him had he not also, as part of his inborn mental equipment, an instinctive propensity to peck—not at everything, but at the sort of things which will nourish him—and an instinctive propensity to launch himself in the air, not at once, but as soon as his wings have grown strong enough to carry him. These propensities, and hundreds more, he has in due time and proportion. His impulses and desires are adjusted to his needs and capacities just as finely as his bodily equipment. He displays, not merely the purposive organisation of a motor-car, but that of a motor-car complete with driver, thoroughly trained and adequately instructed as to the nature of his route. Bearing all this in mind, it seems indeed a desperate hazard to deny that this has been arranged for by some intelligence able both to conceive the design, and to control the material in fulfilment of it.

81.—PURPOSES TRANSCENDING THE INDIVIDUAL

In the main the purpose served by the physical and mental organisation of a living creature is an individual purpose, the maintenance of its own life. But in at least one respect there is also clear indication of a purposive organisation transcending the individual. This is in the relation between members of the same species: The human infant, for instance, is after all not born with a structure and habits immediately well adapted to the preservation of his life. He is born almost entirely helpless, and quite incapable of securing his own survival. Yet provision has been made for securing his survival, not in his structure, but in the structure of a particularly important part of his environment, namely, his mother. As soon as he is born, " nature " takes care to provide in his mother's breasts nourishment perfectly and precisely suited to his needs. More than this ; the mother is not only equipped by nature with the capacity to feed and care for her offspring ; she is also equipped with a supply of maternal tenderness which makes her willing, and often happy to put up with the many discomforts of caring for him and raising him to the point at which he can fend for himself. Here the purposive unit is not the individual organism alone, but the biological complex consisting of child and mother ; and we can hardly avoid adding the father too, for he needs to go out and bring in the prey, the catch, the harvest, or the pay-packet while the mother is tied to the nursery. It is clearer than ever that the purposiveness which could produce this organisation cannot be that of any individual living thing, but must be something more powerful and far-seeing.

It was once customary to extend this kind of interpretation much more widely, and to see, not merely human society, but the whole terrestrial order of living things, as arranged for the convenience of the one superior living thing, man. This naive self-importance has been deflated by increased knowledge, especially increased knowledge of the history of life on the earth. In face of the facts of biological evolution, we can no longer maintain that the world is built up entirely around man and his needs.

82.—EVOLUTIONARY PROGRESS

But this very knowledge presents us with fresh grounds for reading a purpose into nature. For the history of life on earth is a history of progress. It is now well established that this history may be divided into a great many epochs, passing gradually into one another. At each epoch the types of living creature to be found on the earth were to a large extent different from those of earlier epochs, i.e., there has been the development or " evolution " of new forms of life. Of the older forms, while some have died out, others, representing all the main divisions of the animal and vegetable kingdoms, have survived, alongside the new forms.

This development is not a mere variation, but an advance. Every epoch shows us species which are more highly developed for the purpose of living than their predecessors, able to perform more varied activities, or the same activities in a more efficient way. The first forms of life were exceedingly small, with the limited repertoire of achievements possible to a single cell. Later types were huge complex societies of cells, all collaborating in complex performances. Earliest life was confined to the water ; later species mastered the land and the air, first as crawling reptiles, ultimately with the athletic mastery of the cheetah and the swift. The delicate organs of sensation have developed out of a vague general awareness of the environment. The speciality of man has been in the acquisition of a brain larger and more versatile than anything known in previous ages.

This whole general history of advance, not indeed perfectly continuous and unbroken, but taking a broad view of the whole field persistent, without decisive setbacks, this constant tendency to produce more elaborate, capable, versatile, and sensitive living creatures, more adequately aware of their environment and better able to bring it into accord with their wants, all this suggests strongly a persistent purpose at work, a movement towards a goal, or at least in the same general direction. We can say this without making any moral assumptions, or presuming to say that man is in any absolute sense better than the ape or the kangaroo. It seems reasonable to conclude that this persistence in a general line of advance is due to a directedness of the process as a whole, and not the fortuitous result of a number of disconnected changes. We seem, then, to be participants in a world which has not only been planned, but is in process of construction, so that we play a definite part in bringing that plan to realisation.

Man is a recent arrival on the biological scene (a million years old, at most). His biological evolution has perhaps come nearly to an end. But this does not mean the end of evolutionary progress. On the contrary, it has proceeded at an immensely faster rate by transferring itself from the field of physiological structure to that of culture and society. Present generations of men differ from their ancestors, not in the possession of physical organs or aptitudes transmissible by heredity, but in the possession of manufactured goods, and above all of knowledge, handed down from one generation of society to another. The pace of this kind of change is far greater than change in physical structure ever could be. It is patent that human society has enormously increased its knowledge of its environment and its capacity to control it, and so to survive, and to multiply and vary its achievements. When we compare a modern block of flats with a row of mud huts, a modern library with primitive fairy-tales, we see again the urge towards progress finding itself new and more effective channels.

Thus, if we can no longer see mankind as the pinnacle of a divine edifice, we can see him as the culminating achievement of a great effort or adventure. In neither case need we stop at man. The middle ages believed that there were many orders of angels standing in the hierarchy between

man and God. We may well hope that humanity; with all
its imperfections, is not the last word of the process of
evolution, but that there are finer specimens of living
creatures to be produced, perhaps as the result of our efforts
at self-improvement.

83.—THE MECHANIST VIEW OF LIVING THINGS

To all this evidence of purpose in nature, what can the
materialist reply ? In the first place, he can argue that the
assumption of a spiritual cause operating teleologically is
unnecessary, since for each of these phenomena which so
impress the naive contemplator of the " wonders of nature," a
mechanical cause in the material world can be discovered.
For many of these apparently purposive actions he can give
you the material cause in detail, and he hopes to explain
more and more of them as time goes on. The circulation of
the blood works very much like a plumbing installation ;
and its chemical peculiarities follow from its chemical
composition. The human body, he says, works like a machine,
in that, if you know the physical and chemical constitution of
it, you can work out how it will operate. No other causes
than the material are observable, and none need be postulated.
If the facts can be explained by reference to material causes,
there is no need to confuse the issue with speculations about
possible underlying purposes, which we can only guess at.

In this line of argument there is at least one important
truth. Philosophers of an idealist persuasion have often
concluded from their idealistic principles that the activity of
living creatures cannot be understood, or cannot be
adequately understood, on materialist lines, by means of
the analytical technique of modern science. They have
argued that any attempt at discovering the detailed material
causes of spiritual phenomena is tantamount to an attempt to
turn mind into matter, to imprison in the shackles of a
merciless physical law the free will of the Spirit, which
bloweth where it listeth. And so they have opposed and

discredited the scientific investigation of the living body, and still more of the living mind. (In the same spirit, those who believed that weather was the expression of the mood of the gods scorned empirical meteorology, and, if they accepted any principles of weather-forecasting, they were the teleological principles of the astrologers.)

In this they were certainly wrong. An accumulating mass of well attested materialistic explanations of the phenomena of life and mind warns us that, whatever our final philosophical standpoint may be, it behoves us to find out as much as we can about the way in which body and mind work. If we want our babies to survive and be healthy, we had better investigate as carefully as possible both the conditions which affect the supply of milk, and those which affect the supply of mother-love. If these activities are the fulfilment of a purpose, there is no harm, and much good, in finding out by what means that purpose is achieved, so that, if we approve of it, we may help to carry it out more effectively (for it is obvious that, whether or not Nature ever does anything in vain, she does a good many things imperfectly). Preaching, praying, and fasting may be among the useful techniques for the improvement of human character. On the other hand, they may be less effective than an improvement in the fat ration. Only experience will tell us.

This is to say that the acceptance of a teleological explanation of a living process does not rule out an investigation into its mechanical explanation. The two kinds of explanation are not mutually exclusive ; they are complementary. Locomotives are teleological structures, put together by human beings to serve a definite purpose. But a knowledge of the character and aims of George Stephenson does not enable us to drive one ; for that, we must know the way the thing is put together, and the laws of mechanics which determine its behaviour. Thus in setting the mechanical and the teleological explanation at loggerheads, and treating them as mutually exclusive, the idealist philosophers were mistaken.

84.—ITS INADEQUACY

But in that case, the materialist philosophers were equally mistaken in supposing that, by giving a mechanical explanation of vital processes, they had disposed of the need for a teleological one. Indeed, their fondness for comparing the human or animal body to a machine betrays a naiveté on their part not much less glaring than the anthropocentric naiveté of some of their opponents. For of all things in the universe, machines are the most evidently and indisputably teleological, made by mechanics for definite purposes, and deliberately adjusted by the foresight of those mechanics to adapt themselves to foreseen situations so as to produce a desired result. The stronger the analogy between a living body and a machine, the greater the likelihood that it has been planned by a super-mechanic. For it is surely quite absurd to suppose that when you have described the structure and arrangement of parts in a locomotive, and the manner in which one part moves another according to the laws of mechanics, you have said all there is to say about a locomotive. The most important fact about it, the fact which explains why it comes to be arranged in this manner, is the fact that it is intended to pull loads of people and merchandise from one place to another where they happen to be more in demand. Unless you know this, you do not understand what a locomotive is and what it is doing in the world. If (what is by no means certain at this time of day) a living body can be accounted for on the same mechanical lines as a locomotive, this fact would rule out a certain kind of teleological theory— the kind which believes in casual, spasmodic, arbitrary interferences with the functioning of the organism by an outside agency. It would show that, if we are to look for design at all, the design we must look for lies farther back and reaches farther out in nature, that it extends to the distant origins of living things and to the environing material conditions of their survival. But it would be no argument against there being a design at all. The mechanical explanations leave it just as likely that living bodies came into existence by the chance mixing of their material constituents as it is that a locomotive might come into existence as the result of the chance assemblage of some bits of metal.

Thus the philosophy of " mechanism " has no adequate reply to the presumption of design in nature which can reasonably be drawn from the evident adaptedness of living creatures. And eighteenth-century materialism, which relied on this type of argument and on the methods of explanation of the science of physics, had on the whole the worst of the argument against the idealist philosophers. To suppose a complete mechanical explanation of all the activities of the living organism was no less a venture of faith that to suppose the designing intelligence of a God. And the atheists themselves got into the habit (not yet quite obsolete) of simply substituting for an intelligent male God a rather less intelligent but equally designing female whom they called " Nature," and credited with all sorts of " intentions." In order to present a serious alternative to the doctrine of design, Materialism has to show how, in a world without design or purpose, things nevertheless come to be just as though they had been designed for a purpose. Eighteenth-century materialism could only refer vaguely and unconvincingly to the " laws of chance."

85.—DARWIN'S THEORY OF NATURAL SELECTION

But in the nineteenth century a genuine and plausible explanation of the apparent teleology of nature was put on the market with the publication of Darwin's *Origin of Species* in 1859. Darwin's achievement was to provide a real non-teleological alternative to the teleological account of the origin of living forms. For this reason he is one of the foremost influences on the philosophy of the modern world, and a central figure in the fierce late-nineteenth-century controversy between Science and Religion, or more exactly between certain doctrines of the science and of the Christianity of that period.

Darwin's conclusions rested upon a great mass of detailed biological evidence of which it is impossible to give any account here ; later generations have provided a vast deal more. But his main theory can be quite briefly summarised. He assumes, first, the existence of living creatures of some kind, and, second, the fact of Variation, viz., that the offspring of living creatures, while very much like their parents, are not exactly like them ; in the children there sometimes appear characters which differ, usually only in a small way or to a small degree, from those of their parents. Given these assumptions, he sets out to show how the history of the various types of living creatures will be a history of progressive improvement, in the sense of better and better adaptation to the problems of survival in their own particular environment ; that there will be a tendency for later generations to be more efficient in the business of living than earlier generations ; and this without supposing any plan at work to make them more efficient.

The explanation, once Darwin's genius had pointed it out and amassed the evidence in its support, is simple and even obvious. In the effort to survive, it is an observable fact that most living creatures are unsuccessful. The earth contains far too little food, even too little room, for all the animals who are born ; still less can it accommodate and nourish all the seeds which are sown. Most fail to reach maturity. There is therefore competition for the food-supply—what Darwin called the " struggle for existence." In that competition, those animals and plants will succeed which are in one way or another better equipped than their rivals. There are innumerable respects in which a creature may be better equipped than others. The deer specialised in speed of foot to escape attackers ; the lion in the power of his muscles ; the tortoise in his defensive armour ; the camel in his capacity to go for long periods without water ; the insects, individually fragile, in producing so many offspring that a few can be counted on to grow up. Our speciality is our intelligence, which so far has proved the most useful weapon in the biological struggle. The social solidarity and capacity for self-sacrifice for the good of the community which is most conspicuous in the bees and ants, but is also an important characteristic of men, is another powerful factor in the struggle between animal species.

The survival of the better equipped individual means also the birth, growth, and survival of his children. The animal which loses the struggle for existence does not live long enough to leave a family behind him ; his line perishes. Thus the generations of a living species are continually recruited from the better adapted members of that species, and in turn from the better adapted of their children, and so on, so that in a long enough time the whole character of the species may be changed ; the inefficient types die out, and efficient types become the normal.

These superior types originate at first in chance variation. But, having originated by chance, they are preserved and reproduced and made general by the operation of the process which Darwin called " natural selection." Since the differences of parents from children come about by chance, some will be for the better and some for the worse. Those variations which are for the better will be preserved and reproduced ; those which are for the worse will perish. So there will be a progressive improvement in the species.

We must here remember that in this " better " and " worse " there is no moral connotation ; there is nothing particularly virtuous about a camel's hump. The " survival of the fittest " means the survival of the fittest to survive ; they need not be fittest for doing anything else but survive. Nor is " fitness " an absolute term. A creature survives because it is specially able to live in a particular environment, which includes not only a particular climate and vegetation, but also other living creatures which act as food or as predators. This environment is continually changing, and so the qualities required for survival are not the same either for different places on the earth, or for different periods. The success of man is largely due to his capacity, through intelligence, to modify his habits with changes in his circumstances. Thus it is the severest and the most rapidly changing environments which will produce the most rapid advances and the most efficient adaptation in species.

Generally speaking, the Darwinian point of view has prevailed among biologists. Of course, the original opinions of Darwin himself have been greatly modified in detail, particularly now that we know a great deal more than he did about the actual machinery of biological inheritance. But the general outlines of the theory have been confirmed by subsequent investigation. We cannot say for certain that Natural Selection is the only agency at work in the improvement of species ; we cannot, in view of differences of opinion among the experts, be certain that no evolutionary change is due to the inheritance of acquired characters. But we can be sure that Darwin's " natural selection " is by far the most important force at work in changing the biological inheritance of species. What he described has constantly happened, and is still happening (for instance, each generation of the pests on many of our food crops is found more resistant than the previous generation to the poisons with which we spray them).

The Darwinian theory gives a perfectly satisfactory explanation of evolutionary progress, and is sufficient in itself, given Darwin's assumptions, to account for the known cases of such progress. And it also explains, what the teleological type of explanation does much less adequately, the failures of evolution as well as its successes. It explains, not only why some types have become more efficient in the course of generations, but also why others, protected by isolation or some other stroke of good fortune from the competition which is the sole source of improvement, have remained where they were millions of years ago. For it must be emphasised that biological progress is not a universal phenomenon ; it occurs only in some species. And in most types it goes only so far and then comes to a stop.

Darwinism also explains why so many species have not only failed to progress, but have died out altogether. If evolution is a purposive process, it seems wasteful to have gone to so much trouble in evolving the mighty brontosaurus and his numerous impressive relatives, only to discard them and let them perish without descendants. For, as with individuals, so with species, those superior types that become the ancestors of future generations are often few and rare.

Darwinism, again, can explain why adaptation exists ; but it can also readily deal with the fact that adaptation is imperfect. For, if it depends on the occurrence of favourable mutations by chance, the right mutation may never arrive. The theory assures us that, if the right type of adaptive modification turns up by accident, it will be continued and maintain itself, spread and alter the character of the species in which it is found ; but it does not assure us that the right type of adaptive modification will appear. Brontosaurus and dodo had no luck with their accidental mutations ; pithecan-thropus had ; so we are here to tell the tale, and the saurians are not.

The theory of natural selection has, then, given an adequate explanation of the fact of evolutionary progress, in so far as it is a fact, and likewise of the partial nature of this progress, without recourse to the assumption of any inter-vening purposive agency to direct that progress to any goal. It has shown the progress as the result of forces operating without any general purpose in view. A consistent course of development emerges only as the effect of a vast number of separate changes, livings, dyings, and reproducings, each occurring independently of the rest without any overall plan in view.

Along these lines we can also answer the idealist who is impressed by the fact that each living creature is so nicely adapted to the environment which it happens to live in, fish to swim, birds to fly, and spivs to evade the inspector. This is not because a divine providence has placed each individual in the environment that suits him best ; it is because a ruthless competition has eliminated all those types which are unsuited to the environment in which they find themselves. The perfectly adapted creatures whom we observe to-day are the scanty survivors of hordes of others who attempted and failed. There is adaptation because the environment allows nothing to survive which is not adapted. We observe the few successes and ignore the uncounted legions of failures.

As for human history, the progress that can be observed in it has taken place in just those respects in which, on Darwinian assumptions, we should have expected that it would. Those qualities which are useful in the struggle for existence have shown fairly constant improvement ; but in qualities which are of no particular use in assisting individuals or communities to survive and propagate, however valuable they are in themselves, improvement is much less evident. There is no doubt that we are better farmers, better engineers, better organisers, and above all better destroyers of each others' lives than any of our ancestors. But there is serious doubt whether our morals, our art, or our philosophy has shown any comparable improvement on, say, that of the Greeks of Plato's day.

86.—WHAT DARWINISM LEAVES UNEXPLAINED : VARIATION

This, however, is not quite the whole story. For we must remember that the Darwinian theory begins with two assumptions. One is the assumption of a prodigal random variability in the generations of the living. To account for adaptation in organisms as an accidental—that is, undesigned —effect, we must assume that so many variations occur that we can pretty well count on a few of them being adaptive improvements. This variability is assumed and not explained by the theory of natural selection, and it provides the initial material upon which natural selection operates. About the causes of these variations we still know very little. There is

rigin of life itself. Living things look as though they had
een designed for a purpose. If we reject the belief in a
esigner, we must assume that lifeless things can, of themselves,
ake the form of living things, and, further, that they can
ndergo modifications of form, some of which lead to more
ntricate and elaborate kinds of organisation. This assumption,
hat a piece of machinery as intricate as a living body can
ave come into being without intention, is apt to seem very
mprobable. But it is hard to see where we can find any
neasure of the degree of improbability, and so judge whether
: constitutes a really strong reason for belief in a Designer.
We do not know, either what a world would be like that
ad been created by a God, or what a world would be like
hat had not been created by a God " (G. C. Field).

FURTHER READING.

For the biological facts, see, for instance, P. Geddes and J. A. Thomson
-*Evolution*. J. S. Huxley—*Evolution*, is a very thorough survey of the
abject.

For an eighteenth century treatment of the argument, see D. Hume—
ialogues on Natural Religion ; and for a twentieth century one, L. J.
Henderson—*The Fitness of the Environment*.

XI

THEISM AND THE " PROBLEM OF EVIL "

IF THE chance origin of living organisms seems too improbable to be believed, what is the alternative ? It is, of course, not one but many ; we do not have a straight choice between Materialism and one particular brand of theism, such as Christianity, or even theism of any kind. We have no right to jump straight from the premise that living nature cannot be attributed to chance to the conclusion that it must be attributed to God.

All the same, the most familiar, and in many ways the most satisfying answer to the question " What produced the organisation of living things ? " is simply " God." By " God " most people mean something near to the usual definitions of the theologians—a being eternal, all-powerful, all-knowing perfect in goodness as well as in wisdom and power. He is supposed to have created the whole scheme of nature out of nothing by the pure exercise of His will. It is because He is an intelligent and therefore a designing mind that it betrays evidence of His designs ; it is because He is good, and His creatures in some measure share His goodness, that all things in their degree tend towards good. In many types of religious thought, God is considered especially as the master-planner the Demiurge who fashions the world, the source of order and system in nature. The world is the working-out of a single consistent pattern or plan ; there is one master-plan in which everything created has its appointed place ; there is " one far-off divine event to which the whole creation moves " ; and, though the creatures in the exercise of their freedom may sometimes fall short of their assignment, yet being the work of a perfectly wise Planner, the plan is a perfect plan, and this world the best of all possible worlds, otherwise God would have designed a better.

This assumption certainly gives us an explanation of the unity of the world, and of the existence of design and pattern in it. But it seems to me to explain too much. It postulates a design or plan more perfect and more harmonious than we have any good warrant for discerning in the world. It faces, in fact, two very serious difficulties.

90.—THE DESIGN IS IMPERFECT

(1) The design, however wonderful, however much beyond the power of human intelligence to conceive or of human strength to carry out, is yet in many respects manifestly imperfect. The purposes which we can trace in the organisation of living things are not completely carried out. The perfectly healthy body is an unknown phenomenon in nature. Eyes are myopic and astigmatic, glands are over- or under-active, teeth decay ; every individual we know has some organic weakness which prevents the purpose of full, vigorous, happy life from being completely achieved. If wild nature has a better standard of health than civilised men, that is because a ruthlessly high death-rate weeds out all sub-standard individuals before they reach maturity ; it is a result of competition, not of planning.

In a dry year the corn dies, and it is only up-to-date human organisation which prevents us from dying too. With our puny strength and limited vision, we have never-theless managed to improve on " nature " in a good many respects, and to produce artificial tools with a higher degree of reliability than anything which grows naturally. Motor-cars are a better means of propulsion than horses, and adding-machines better arithmeticians than the natural man. The case is just as plain if we take moral rather than physical perfection to be the main purpose of creation ; for it is clear that a man born with a strong tendency to alcoholism or morbid depression or fits of ungovernable rage is no better equipped for the achievement of moral perfection than a man born with one leg longer than the other is equipped for athletic perfection.

Because of this imperfection of adjustment between aim and capacity, terrestrial life is full of frustration, of pain, sorrow, and defeat. There is no need to give instances, or to try to measure the vastness of the failure and suffering in the world. This imperfection, this incessant failure and frustration of aim, does not look like the work of an omnipotent and benevolent Creator. It seems impossible that Omnipotence could be so bungling. So many projects are started which are never finished ; the industrious and devoted mother-insect lays eggs by the million, whereof perhaps half-a-dozen, perhaps none at all, will ever reach maturity (it is the same with the human production of spermatozoa). Anyone who coolly regards the world as the work of a Designer with absolutely unlimited power can hardly avoid the feeling that he could have made a better job of it himself. If there is such an omnipotent Creator, there is little to suggest that His designs are benevolent, and a good deal to indicate a large streak of cruelty in His character. At any rate, He seems to worry little how much unhappiness is involved in the carrying out of His plans.

But the indications of design in the world give us no good ground for believing in such an omnipotent Master. There is only evidence for the partial and imperfect fulfilment of many designs, for an approximation in this sublunary sphere, as Plato saw it, to the eternal forms or patterns which perhaps are perfectly exemplified in a better world than this.

91.—NO UNITY OF PURPOSE IN NATURE

(2) There is unity in nature, and there is purpose in nature. But there is very little indication in nature of unity of purpose. Each individual living creature has his own purposes, and these are in continual conflict with the purposes of other individuals. The wolf is an admirably designed

machine for tracking down, catching, and dismembering sheep ; that is to say, for frustrating the purposes of chewing grass, growing wool, and producing lambs for which the sheep is equally admirably designed.   If the wolf and the sheep form part of the same plan, it is, as Heraclitus long ago perceived, a pattern of conflict which they carry out.   As they stand, the purposes of wolf and sheep are incompatible ; they cannot both be achieved together, or form part of the same system of ends.   If either of them fits into the one general purpose of nature, the other does not, and has no business to be there at all.   Similarly, some of the most beautiful examples of adaptive design are found among the parasites, who live by killing their hosts, or by making their lives a misery.   Materially and mechanically the world is one ; but purposively, so far as we can see, it is inescapably many and diverse.   On the strength of this evidence, there is more to be said than we usually admit for the theory of polytheism, the existence of many, sometimes conflicting, superhuman purposes, for the ancient idea that there is a god of the wolves and a god of the sheep, but no god of the whole animal creation.

THE " PROBLEM OF EVIL "

That the world is guided and sustained by a God who is not only powerful but all-powerful, not only all-powerful but benevolent, or at any rate just, is a belief which very many people for many reasons have greatly desired to hold. A God who is not omnipotent might fail to accomplish something which seems to you of vital importance ; a God ill-disposed or indifferent to human happiness might even deliberately frustrate it.   And so, many ingenious arguments have been devised to explain, or to explain away, the facts in the make-up of the world which seem to conflict with this belief.   The conflict between the belief and the facts produces what is traditionally called " the problem of evil."   For all of us there is a " problem of evil " of a kind, namely, how to get rid of it, but this particular problem arises only for those who believe in a God both omnipotent and benevolent.

92.—THE ARGUMENT THAT EVIL IS NOTHING REAL

The quickest way of disposing of the evils and imperfections in the world is to argue that for the existence of evil no explanation is required : for, evil consisting merely in the absence of good, the absence of something which would be an improvement if it were present is in itself nothing at all ; and, being in itself nothing, requires no cause or explanation. In so far as a thing exists and is real, it is good. God is the cause of this positive being, which is good. But, since evil has no positive being, but consists merely in the thing's lacking some other goodness which it might have possessed, evil is not caused by God or by anything else ; there is nothing there to cause.

This argument is a mere quibbling with words. For, even if you can manage to convince yourself that pain, for instance, is nothing but the absence of pleasure—and to me it seems there can be nothing in the world more definite and positive than pain—the argument is still a quibble. If I make coffee, and deliberately put no sugar in it, am I not responsible for the bitter taste ? The sugarlessness, if you like, is nothing actual or positive ; but the making of the sugarless coffee, the putting together of the ingredients so as to produce a brew with that particular taste, is an actual and positive event of which I am the author, and I am properly blamed if you do not like the taste of it. There is a choice I make between putting sugar in and leaving it out. So, if an almighty God created the world just as it is, He is responsible for leaving out what He left out as well as for putting in what He put in.

93.—THE ARGUMENT THAT EVIL IS ONLY APPARENT

There is a less cavalier treatment of the difficulty which is more commonly met with in the religious apologetics of all periods. The argument runs along these lines. There are undoubtedly many things in the world which appear to us to be evil. But this is an appearance only, due to our imperfect understanding, which again is due to the fact that we apprehend only a fragment of the whole universe. If we could comprehend the whole scheme of Reality and its complete pattern and purpose at once, we should see that every element in it makes its contribution to a universal harmony, a universal plan ; the apparent evils are necessary parts of a whole which is as perfect as possible, and in the light of a perfect knowledge would appear not evil but good.

This argument is a kind of philosophical confidence trick. We are asked to believe that, in spite of his shabby appearance, the share-pusher really has a fabulously rich gold mine in some foreign country which, unfortunately, it is impossible for us to visit. That is to say, the theory, getting no support from the facts which everyone can observe, is given support by an appeal to another set of alleged facts which nobody can observe. For it is impossible for us to achieve this comprehensive view in which cancer and civil war, waste and frustration, appear good and necessary to the economy of the universe.

When a man rests his theory on assertions which nobody can verify, it is impossible to refute him. But, for the same reason, there are no grounds for believing him. There is no way of proving our theologians' case, or even of making it plausible. There is no evidence for the existence of any cosmic purpose which might require pain, deformity, stupidity, strife, hate, and sorrow for its fulfilment. There is evidence of purposes in the world, but of purposes which, aiming at health and strength and happiness, are often not fulfilled.

And even if we accept the hypothesis on which this argument proceeds, I am not sure that it faces the issues squarely. For if *from our point of view* many things seem evil, our point of view with all its miseries and imperfections is still part of the universe, and we cannot escape from it. Perhaps if we were other than we are able to be, we should not mind. But, being as we are, we do mind, and our minding is an evil—a real evil, for here the distinction between real and apparent does not apply ; suffering is what it feels like, and is nothing but the feeling.

94.—THE ARGUMENT THAT EVIL IS DUE TO SIN

There is a third way of side-stepping this " problem of evil." This is to say that the evil in the world is the consequence, not of the will of God, but of the will of His creatures ; or, sometimes, of only one type of creature, viz., man. This doctrine has some support from the early chapters of the book of Genesis, where the blame is further narrowed down to the two individuals Adam and Eve—or three, if you count the serpent. God could, of course, say these theorists, have avoided the evil by refraining from giving us free will ; but to give us free will, with all its possibilities for evil, was still better than to make us automata who always did the right thing because we couldn't help it.

I think this would be a fair solution to the problem if we could allow its assumptions. But note what those assumptions are. We must suppose that every untoward event in the world throughout all its history is the result of the free choice of some human being or other created free agent ; and that it was the best possible arrangement, not only to endow us with a freedom of choice bound to issue in great evils, all of which God foresaw, but to assign to these choices immense capacity for causing suffering to ourselves and to the rest of His creatures. And when one says that God *could not* have made a world of free men except at the cost of so much suffering, the doctrine of His omnipotence wears a somewhat equivocal aspect. But however this may be, the theory must, I think, be written off as another form of the confidence trick. For, while a great deal of the evil in the world is certainly the result of human choice, most of it, as far as we can see, is not. No depravity of will produces earthquakes and floods and droughts, the cancerous growth, the tubercle bacillus, the pains of childbirth.

As for the view that these evils are inflicted on us as retribution for the misdeeds of certain of our ancestors or of our contemporaries, I do not think this crude and repulsive theory is worth discussing, in spite of the fact that many upright men have managed to make themselves believe it. A God as mean and vindictive as this, who punishes men in the mass for the misdeeds of individuals, has no claim to the epithet " good."

The supposition that each man is being punished for *his own* sins (though his punishment seems to begin very early in life) is of course yet another form of the confidence trick. For if Job is known to be an upright man in public, one can always allege, as his three friends did, that he has horrible vices in private. Or, when this is too unplausible, one can say that he committed them in a previous existence. This is not impossible ; but there is no reason whatever to believe it.

XII

THE EVIDENCE OF RELIGIOUS EXPERIENCE

95.—RELIGIOUS EXPERIENCE

I HAVE found the traditional arguments for the existence of God somewhat unconvincing. And in fact, it is unlikely that very many people have come to believe in God as a result of hearing arguments of this kind. The belief in God is transmitted in the main, not by argument, but by the testimony of those who claim to have had direct experience of His reality. And if theism is to be fairly considered, this claim must receive some attention.

It is made on the grandest and fullest scale by those who call themselves mystics, whose unusual experiences have been achieved as the result of a long and arduous course of mental, emotional, and physical discipline, often involving considerable suffering. It is made in a more modest and tentative manner by great numbers of ordinary worshippers living normal lives, in which the practice of prayer plays a part ; and their experiences may come ordinarily, even casually, in the normal business of living. Both the intense and abnormal mystical experiences, and the quieter and more ordinary kind, have been enjoyed by individuals of many divergent religious faiths. No church is without its mystics, and no theology is independent of the influence of their teaching.

Sometimes the alleged illumination of the mystical state relates to specific doctrines of particular religions. And since these doctrines are often incompatible with each other, it is clear that mystical illumination is not infallible, and error sometimes, at least, occurs in it. But amongst a good deal of diversity in the interpretation of experiences which the mystics themselves admit to be difficult to interpret, there is a central core of doctrine upon which mystics of all faiths are fairly well agreed.

They say that it is possible for man, for short periods and on rare occasions, to have an awareness of an independent reality which is not gained through the senses. This awareness is clear and certain, and sweeps away all doubt. It is an awareness of a being, God, other than the man, and yet in intimate communion with him ; infinitely greater than the man in every respect, and yet, as a spiritual being, not altogether alien. The nature of God is best described by negations : no sensory descriptions will apply to Him, no terms of human psychology are adequate to His nature ; to those who lack the intuition of His presence, He must remain inconceivable. But He is known to be related to the rest of the universe as its one source or ground of being ; He is the one ultimate reality. In consequence, all beings in the universe are united by this common dependence upon the one God ; the whole world partakes of a common nature, and pulses to a common rhythm. Of this united whole of reality, the individual man is an infinitesimal part or phase ; but, in so far as he draws his being from the eternal and infinite being, he in his own measure partakes of the nature of the infinite and eternal.

The feeling of the mystic in the presence of God is in the first place a sense of his own dependence upon God, of his own weakness and imperfection before the divine power and majesty, hence a feeling of awe, of self-contempt and self-abasement, with reverence for God. In the second place, it is a feeling of love and trust : the worshipper loves God, feels that His purposes are good and His power beyond challenge, so that, placing himself in God's hands, he has a perfect and ultimate security. Thus the claim of religious experience is that there exists an " infinite " Being upon whom all finite beings are dependent, and that men may directly know this Being by means of a spiritual communion. In the more advanced stages of mystical experience, one no longer hears of communion, but of union ; the worshipper is absorbed into the being of God, and is one with Him.

A further claim is added to this. In communion with God, there is not merely an awareness, but the transmission of a spiritual influence. Prayer and the mystic state are sources of power ; the practice of the presence of God makes a difference to the personality, the sentiments and the actions of the worshipper. This influence is for the better. The man who has enjoyed communion with the divine derives from that communion a profound sense of security, which makes him master of his fears, relatively careless of what misfortunes may befall him in the transient phenomenal world, and so able to act generously or heroically without being deterred by fear of the consequences. Sometimes, indeed, he claims that so long as he puts his trust in God, he is assisted by providence—that is, circumstances seem to be adjusted to his needs as they arise ; but in any case the belief that he is in God's care gives him courage to deal with all difficulties. There is an increase of spiritual power ; the man feels himself to draw on resources not normally open to him. This may extend to the exercise of abnormal powers such as the power to cure disease by " faith " or to the spectacular endurance of physical sufferings beyond what would be normally bearable. But more usually it means a greater peace of mind, a greater self-command in the fulfilment of accepted moral ideals. The religiously experienced person is released from the drag of petty interests and free to pursue the " higher " ends of life. He possesses a single-minded concentration on that purity of heart which will bring him closer to God. Recognising that he himself is only part of a world-wide whole, and seeking to conform his will to the comprehensive will of God, he will love others as fellow-sharers in the divine nature, and will their good as readily as he wills his own.

The religious are of one mind in holding that the knowledge of God is not to be had except at a price. That price is that the man shall give up his self-interest, his predominant concern with his own physical organism and its biological prosperity, his own psychical organism and its achievements and status in human society ; he shall, as far as he is able, seek no satisfactions for himself except the satisfaction of knowing God and carrying out His will. His individual personality is reckoned as unimportant ; it is to be subordinated to a greater personality which takes control.

96.—IS IT AN ILLUSION ?

Now, what value are we to attach to religious experiences of this kind as indications of the nature of ultimate reality ? One alternative is to regard them as entire illusions, giving us no valid information about anything except the state of mind of the persons who enjoy them. This is a reasonable view, and it may be the true one. The states of mind of mystics are abnormal, in somewhat the same fashion in which the states of mind of opium-eaters or persons under anæsthetics are abnormal. We know that opium-eaters and anæsthetised persons often have interesting and exciting experiences, which we have every reason to believe are completely illusory. It may be so with mystical experiences, too ; and with some aspects of these experiences it is very probably so.

As for the religious experiences that come in more normal states of consciousness, we can easily discern, in the persons who have them, certain strong emotional needs which might well produce these experiences spontaneously, though there were nothing outside to cause them. Sudden uprushes of feeling, of joy, trust, and love, of the relief of a pre-existing emotional tension, may very well occur through the operation of psychological forces within the personality itself. There is nothing illusory about the feelings themselves, but there is illusion in so far as the subject attributes these feelings to the intervention of the divine—having, no doubt, been taught by his religious teachers to do so. Religious conversion (like romantic falling-in-love) tends to happen especially to those who have been led to expect it.

It is true that, for the experient himself, experiences of this kind have a force and conviction which is irresistible ; he is often unable to doubt of the truth of what has been revealed to him. But firm subjective conviction is, unfortunately, no guarantee of objective truth. The strongest convictions may be mistaken. Indeed, the unusual firmness of a conviction is sometimes an indication of its irrational origin ; some of the most confident and unshakeable assurances of truth are enjoyed by the inhabitants of lunatic asylums.

There is, then, some plausibility in the view that whatever is revealed in religious experience is illusion. But, while we may have in the end to dismiss all this evidence as worthless for our purpose of understanding the universe, I think it would be very rash to dismiss it without very careful and respectful consideration. If the ability of man to know God is an illusion, it is a very widespread illusion. The mystics, unlike the opium-eaters, are to a great extent consistent with themselves and with each other in their accounts of what they learn through their peculiar experiences. These accounts have the *prima facie* claim to a hearing which is the right of every human cognitive experience until it is proved invalid.

Nor is religious experience especially associated with any particular kind of craziness or weakness of mind. Mystics are sometimes odd ; the same may be said of eminent scientists. But they also count among their number many men of profound intellect and great practical shrewdness, especially in the understanding of human character and motives. We are not entitled to ignore what they say because we find their persons uncongenial, or their manner of life unattractive.

97.—PRACTICAL VALUE OF RELIGIOUS EXPERIENCE

In considering their interpretation of the world, we must first notice that it has two aspects, a practical and a theoretical. Before all else, religion is a way of living, and its primary concern is to show men how to conduct their lives. The practical claim of religious people is that those who live devoutly, seeking the presence of God in prayer, and trying to subject their wills to His purposes, find thereby strength. and peace in their everyday lives.

This claim cannot be discussed at length here. It is evident that many people do achieve by this way of life a harmonious adjustment of their personalities to their circumstances, and succeed in living with greater self-control and peace of mind through a religious faith than they could without one. But it is not evident that this method will be a success with everybody, or that it is the only effective way of attaining psychological health.

In any case, whereas the practical effectiveness of the religious way of life adds some confirmation to the theoretical claims of religion, it is very far indeed from proving them. The fact that a belief has a good effect on the life of the believer does nothing to show that this belief is true (whatever some pragmatists may say in unguarded moments). The good results that follow from religious experience and religious faith as regards the happiness and efficiency of the believer may well be due purely to psychological developments within his soul, to the resolution of conflict and the release of fresh energies within himself, and not at all to the intervention of " divine grace " from outside. One may accept all that religious people claim for their faith as a successful manner of living, and at the same time deny that their belief in God is true.

Indeed some philosophers have suggested that the practical teaching of religion is its whole meaning ; " God " to them is a name, not for a transcendent being, but for the capacity of human beings to live more whole-heartedly and more lovingly. But if that were indeed all that was meant by the existence of God, belief in Him would fail of its effect. Whatever good effects religion has, come about because men believe in the power and help of a God who is not just themselves.

98.—ITS THEORETICAL CLAIMS

There remains, then, the theoretical claim ; that in religious experience men know the existence of God. I have granted this claim a *prima facie* plausibility. But if it is to be made good, it must not stop at the bare and vague assertion that God can be known. It must produce some account of the relation between the ultimate divine Reality known in religious experience, and the ordinary lesser realities known in other kinds of experience. It must fit God and the rest of the known world into a system of ideas which makes at least some coherent sense. In so far as the knowledge of the mystic is really ineffable and incommunicable, it is of no use to the philosopher.

In this process of fitting together the findings of religious experience and those of scientific investigation, science must take precedence over religion. Where there is a clear conflict between a dogma of religion and a well-attested scientific law, the dogma must give way. (This rule does not, of course, give any special weight to the opinions of scientists on matters outside their scientific studies). Many doctrines once considered essential parts of Christianity (for instance, those concerning the origin of the human species) have had to make this surrender. For the scientists are able to confirm their conclusions by countless successful predictions. And the verification of scientific laws can be carried out by all of us in our ordinary experience, and not only by some of us in occasional extraordinary experiences arrived at after a long course of prayer and fasting. Only the scientist has any right to the motto *Securus judicat orbis terrarum*.

99.—THE WORLD AS A SPIRITUAL UNITY

Now the first article of the mystical creed is that the universe is fundamentally one ; that there is a single source or basis of all reality underlying the diversity of things. This conviction is expressed in various kinds of theoretical anguage, ranging from the downright assertions of the Hindu Upanishads, that everything is identical with everything else, to the Christian image of one omnipotent and omnipresent Father and Ruler of all ; but no mystic fails to assert it and to emphasize it, even when he is an adherent of a polytheistic religion, such as the Hindu or the Greek. Only the One is completely and eternally real, and from the One all things are derived.

This principle does not in itself conflict with the findings of science, but rather finds confirmation there. As we have already seen, there is plenty of scientific evidence for an underlying unity among the world's diversities. The laws of nature form one system. If we call this underlying unity Matter when we are considering its articulation in minute local and temporary processes, may we not, like Spinoza, call it God when we consider it in its eternal and universal completeness ? We need not be surprised if we possess, in the mystical consciousness, an awareness of the fundamental unity, while in other forms of consciousness we are aware of various aspects of the diversity.

But religion goes beyond science in maintaining that the ultimately real One is a spiritual being. God is not, indeed, just a large-size man, or just a perfect man ; thought, feeling, will in Him cannot be of the same kind as they are in us. Nevertheless, attributes analogous to these on a higher level do belong to God, and we may speak of Him in psychological terms without talking nonsense. If, then, the religious consciousness is to contribute towards the philosophical understanding of reality, we must find some intelligible account of the relation of this supreme spirit to the rest of the universe. In what manner is the world derived from an ultimate spiritual unity ?

Religious answers to this question are apt to be given largely in myth and metaphor, not easily translated into plain terms. If any form of mystical doctrine is the truth, this is to be expected. God is a unique being, and his relation to the world a unique relation, which cannot, therefore, be

precisely defined in terms applying to the relations between
other things with which we are familiar.   The best we can
hope for is an analogy which will hint at the essential feature
of the relation.   Bearing this in mind, we find that religious
doctrines fall into two groups.

100.—" TRANSCENDENCE "

One type of doctrine stresses the distinctness of God from
the world ; He is not a part of the world but " transcends "
it.   The relation between the two is a one-sided dependence
the world owes all its being to the power of God, while His
nature is unchanged by anything that happens in the world
God is imagined in the guise of a maker or designer of the
universe, bringing it into existence and controlling its destinies
by acts of will ; or as a ruler, issuing commands to lesser
beings, backed by promises of rewards and threats of
punishments.   Most Christians have thought of God in this
fashion.

If the metaphors of " creation " and " lordship " are to
contribute to our understanding of the relation of God to
the world, they must imply that the world is the product of
a single irresistible purpose.   The difficulties of interpreting
the course of nature in this manner have already been
considered.   If, despite appearances, the world does
consistently carry out a single purpose, there is little ground
for believing that the divine purpose is at all in accordance
with our purposes, or is much concerned with the individual
welfare of the creatures.

101.—" IMMANENCE "

The other type of religious doctrine is that in which
God is not separate from the world, but present or " immanent "
in it.   The world's unity is not that of an externally imposed
pattern, but that of an inward life.   God, or the Absolute
Spirit, is not the greatest Being ; He is the whole of Being ;

He comprehends the world ; being infinite, He has nothing outside Him which might limit Him. All the universe is one and the same reality appearing in diverse forms. In appearance, from our partial and inadequate point of view, it is many : in reality, from the universal point of view which is that of God, it is one.

This type of doctrine, according to which all things have their being in God, expresses the mystic's awareness of his complete absorption and union with the divine being. It is especially characteristic of the philosophy of India, where this mystical experience has been most intensively cultivated. In Europe, the philosophies of Spinoza and Hegel belong to the same type. " Pantheism " is the general term for this type of philosophy.

102.—CAN MANY MINDS MAKE UP ONE MIND?

If a theory of this kind is the truth, we must suppose that in some way or other many small, limited minds can be included in and form parts of one great, unlimited mind. This is not a state of affairs of which we have any direct experience, as we have of the way in which several small objects in space may form part of one large object in space. In what way can we conceive of the union of many souls to make one ? At first sight the answer may seem simple enough. My mind comprises an awareness of a small section of the whole world-process—at the moment of writing, it is limited to some of the events taking place inside one particular room. Your mind comprises an awareness of another section. The Absolute or divine mind will be aware of the whole world-process at once, including all the awarenesses of all the finite minds. Whereas our consciousnesses are fragmentary, its consciousness would be complete. And perhaps limitations of time as well as of space would disappear in it, and it would comprehend all the past and all the future in one eternal act of intuition.

But there are serious difficulties in this conception. My awareness is essentially an awareness of limitations. I am conscious of the boundaries of my field of vision ; of my own ignorance of many facts ; of my distinctness and separateness from you. To remove this limitedness is at once to alter the character of my experience. Wondering, doubting, learning, are normal features of my experience ; but how could they belong to an experience which already knew everything there is to be known ? Those elements at least which are consequent upon the finiteness of my experience can hardly be reproduced in an infinite experience. And indeed pantheistic philosophers commonly maintain that the imperfections of finite experience have no place in the Absolute or the mind of God. For instance, many philosophers hold that space and time are forms belonging to a limited and partial experience ; and the divine experience is not, like ours, spatial and temporal. But if this is so, if there are characteristics of finite experience which do not belong to the infinite experience, then we cannot say that the infinite experience includes or consists of or is identical with the finite experiences. There may perhaps be a mind which is aware of all the things that you and I and all other people are aware of ; but if so, it is a different mind from yours and mine and everybody else's ; it does not consist of these various separate minds in combination. To be aware of the same objects as I am is not to be me.

A different sort of difficulty arises when we remember, what philosophers are sometimes disposed to forget, that a mind is not a mere contemplator of events, but a feeler and doer as well. A mind which includes me must include my emotions, desires, and decisions as well as my sensations and ideas. A mind which includes all humanity must include the feelings and resolves of the Jews about the Arabs, and the feelings and resolves of the Arabs about the Jews, and feel and will them as its own. It must then contain innumerable inner discords and clashes of purpose, feeling mutually discordant emotions and willing mutually inconsistent courses of action. Is there any good sense in calling such a welter of antagonisms one personality? If so, it looks as though this personality must suffer from a more extreme kind of mental conflict and dissociation than the worst cases in our lunatic asylums.

In the mystical experience itself, there is little warrant for such an interpretation. The mystic does not become aware of everything that goes on in the world; it seems rather as though he is aware of nothing that goes on in the world. Far from embracing the experiences of others, his state of mind is sometimes soberly described as an experience of nothing. And to reach it, he has to abandon his ordinary experiences, his everyday sensations, thoughts, and emotions altogether.

Further, while this type of theory tries to accommodate itself to one aspect of religious experience, the consciousness of unity with the divine, it fails to take adequate account of another equally prominent aspect of religious experience. Religious persons of all types and persuasions usually act upon the assumption that God has preferences, enjoins moral standards upon his worshippers, approves the good and condemns the evil; some actions are well-pleasing to Him, and others are not. It is not easy to find a religious faith that is not associated with an ethical programme.

But if we are to hold that God is everything that exists, and does everything that is done, then everything alike is holy and according to the divine will; the criminal and the lunatic fulfil their aspect of the divine nature, and are as they must be. In the sight of God, the distinction between good and evil disappears; it exists only for the limited interests and viewpoints of finite souls. (Spinoza is clear and consistent on this point). So it is hard to see how a pantheistic God can prefer one course of action to another, can approve the good and condemn the evil. The religious idea of the moral responsibility of man towards God cannot well find a place in a consistent pantheist philosophy. Indeed, the most celebrated expression of Hindu pantheism, the Bhagavad-Gita, does give the impression of teaching that it is foolish and impious to be concerned about the consequences of your actions. Pantheistic philosophers have, of course, given us much profound and moving moral teaching. But to suggest that any course of action is more God-like or dearer to God than any other does involve giving up the strict identification of God with the whole of reality.

I have mentioned two patterns by which we may think of the relation between God and ourselves. The first is the pattern of Creation, whereby God is conceived after the fashion of a craftsman or artist making the world, but, unlike human makers, making the materials as well as imposing a form upon them, and so not restricted, like human makers, by the character of those materials. Such a God is outside the world and in no way dependent on it, while it is entirely dependent on Him. To this I have objected that the existence of innumerable imperfections in the world, i.e., things contrary to those purposes and ideals we can discern in it, and of innumerable conflicts and frustrations of purpose, does not accord with the picture of a Creator who is complete master of His materials, and is carrying out through them a single consistent plan.

The second pattern is that of Composition, whereby God is conceived as identical with the world taken as a unitary whole, particular existents being parts or aspects of the divine being. To this I have objected that the adding or fusing of all finite experiences together would not make a divine personality. Is there any other pattern by which we can think of the relation between God and ourselves?

103.—RELATION BETWEEN SOUL AND BODY

If we wish to understand how the divine mind operates in the world, we are most likely to be helped by considering how our own minds do so. A human mind works in the world through its association with a human body. As to the nature of this association, older philosophies often thought of the body as a receptacle and an instrument for the soul ; inserting itself into the body like a chauffeur getting into a car, the soul proceeded to direct the body according to its will. That is, the body is held to be quite different in nature from the soul ; it is inert unless impelled by the soul ; and it is, or may be, entirely the servant of the soul.

These principles are mistaken. When we have removed the confusion between the body, as a complex of physical processes, and the set of sense-data through which those processes are perceived,* the proper distinction between " body " and " mind " or " soul " becomes clear. This distinction is necessary because, of the processes which together make up a human organism, there are some which the individual is aware of and can consciously control, and others which he cannot. The body is a system of vital activities outside the person's consciousness, but intimately connected with his conscious activities. In this sense, the body is not different in nature from the soul ; body and soul form a single purposive system and share the same ends, habits, and character. The body is not an inert instrument, but pursues its own characteristic activities while the soul sleeps or is attending to something else. The body is not and cannot be completely under the control of the soul—there are many bodily activities with which the conscious will cannot interfere ; and, while conscious decision modifies the activities of the body, the body in turn provides impulses which direct the activity of the conscious mind.

The relation between soul and body is like that between the administrative and the executive grades of an organisation. The general direction of policy is the concern of the soul. I myself decide on what main lines of activity the energies of my organism are to be expended. But the routine maintenance of the organism's life, and the detailed execution of my general intentions, are matters which I leave to the body to carry out by itself. This is true, not only of the inherited dispositions of the body, in whose formation my consciousness

*See Secs. 64 and 65.

has no part, but also of the acquired dispositions called habits : the process of habit-formation involves a devolution to the body of functions which were originally the work of the soul.

So much, common-sense can observe for itself. Biology tells us more. The bodies of all animals except the very simplest are, we are told, not just single organisms, but societies of organisms. My body is made up of many millions of cells ; and each of these cells is of itself a living organism, possessing an organic structure of its own, and performing for itself all the essential functions of life—feeding, digesting, excreting, growing, etc. The whole organism began its existence as a single cell, and the millions of which it is now composed have all developed from that one cell by a series of divisions of one cell into two. Each group of cells has its own peculiar structure and activities ; and each makes a necessary contribution towards maintaining the total form and activity of the whole organism.

We may say that the life of the human being and that of the cells are one and the same thing. The man does nothing which is not the act of some group of cells, or of them all at once. In a sense, the man *is* his cells. And yet he is quite unaware of the very existence of all these separate lives which together sustain his life, until some biologist apprises him of the fact.

It is not unplausible to attribute a kind of conscious experience to each individual cell, seeing that there are some animals which consist of only one cell, and there is no sharp dividing-line between these and multicellular animals. But these cell-consciousnesses certainly do not combine to constitute the total consciousness of the human person ; he is unaware of the matters which must constitute the main concern of any consciousness which the cell may have.

Here, then, we have an observable pattern of one-in-many, a fashion in which the activities of one living thing can involve, can in a sense consist of, the activities of many lesser, subordinate living things. This is the way a human personality operates in the world, fulfilling itself through the operation of countless inferior organisms, which its own activity has produced to supply its own needs.

104.—GOD AS THE SOUL OF THE WORLD

Now, if we are to suppose that the human soul is not the highest form of personality in existence, but that there is a divine soul, or more than one, far exceeding our own in knowledge and power, I think that this is the most promising analogy we can use for understanding the relation between Him and ourselves. It gives us, at any rate, one way in which we can think of ourselves as standing in a subordinate relation to a divine personality.

Applying this analogy, we may suppose that there is a vaster vital activity to which the life of individual men and animals contributes, a more comprehensive purpose which our actions may help to fulfil. There is a supreme mind which forms these vaster purposes and directs their execution. But the divine plans are effected through the acts of subordinate beings ; there are no separate " acts of God," as distinct from the acts of His creatures. The activity of the creatures is to some extent independent of the will of God ; thus the control of God over the world, like the control of the soul over the body, is imperfect. The various orders of living creatures may be regarded as offspring of the divine life, expressing various aspects of the divine intention. There would then be a continuity of nature between the lesser personality and the great personality from which it issued. And we might suppose that, besides the superficial level of consciousness in which the individual is aware of his own distinct identity, purposes, and circumstances, there is a deeper level in which he is aware of his own ultimate identity with God, and through Him with all other creatures.

Such a theory fits fairly well the testimony of religious experience. If that experience is valid, it requires at least that there should be a supreme Mind or Spirit, far exceeding our own in its powers, but sufficiently like ourselves to be called Mind or Spirit ; that there is for each of us a course of action which expresses the divine will, which we may become aware of, and may or may not carry out ; that we are dependent upon God for our very being ; that somehow or other we may become united with God, so that He dwells within us, and that thereby we achieve the most complete fulfilment of our personalities ; that in God all things are one, and in His purposes all are united. If we take religious experience as conveying truth about the nature of reality, and therefore try to interpret the universe as the manifestation of one supreme spirit, this type of theory, regarding God as the soul of the universe, seems to me most likely to give an acceptable explanation.

FURTHER READING.

W. James—*Varieties of Religious Experience*.
E. Underhill—*Mysticism*.
For Hindu pantheism, the *Bhagavad-Gita*.
The most famous expression of European pantheism is B. Spinoza—*Ethics*.

XIII

CONCLUSIONS

OUR results so far have been mainly negative. None of
the philosophies so far considered has been found to
prove its case. It is time to see whether any conclusions
can be drawn from our discussion. Our principal topic has
been what is commonly called the relation between Mind
and Matter. I think that this way of stating the problem is
rather misleading, in so far as it suggests that Mind and
Matter are two distinct things or substances, somehow
externally connected with one another. I have argued that,
on the contrary, to be mental (i.e., to possess consciousness
and whatever goes with consciousness) and to be material
(i.e., to have position and motion, and to cause other things
to move, in physical space) are not incompatible
characteristics, but the same thing or process may possess
both. In fact, there is quite good evidence that all mental
processes are also material, i.e., involve the motion of mass
and the transfer of energy. But there is no good evidence for
the converse proposition, the principle of Idealism, that all
material processes are also mental. On the contrary, the
appearances strongly suggest that most material processes in
the world belong to no mind, since they do not display any
trace of that purposive adaptiveness which is the mark of
mentality. It appears, then, that the world contains both
things or processes which are conscious and purposive, and
things or processes which are not.

There need be no problem about the co-existence in
one world of the mental and the non-mental. Nor need we
find anything puzzling in the fact that minds sometimes
affect and are affected by other things which are not minds.
But a problem does arise when we consider facts of two kinds.

(1) The mental appears to come into existence without any other cause or origin than the non-mental ; Not-Mind not only affects but apparently *produces* Mind by itself. This seems to have happened in the early history of the earth, when an entirely inorganic world was succeeded by one containing intelligent living creatures, with no discoverable outside interference. And it is still happening constantly, by the transformation of inorganic matter into organic forms, and of the lower and doubtfully mental organisms into higher and indisputably mental organisms. Are we to suppose that what is not mind can *become* mind ? And if so, what else must we suppose to make the transformation credible ?

(2) Non-mental processes are not limited to the inorganic world. There are activities of all living organisms, including the highest, which are precisely analogous to the behaviour of inorganic matter, and can be explained by the same physical laws. The organism is only partly mental, and in many of its activities consciousness has no part. Yet soul and body, the mental and the non-mental, are not merely in contact with each other, but are united into a single whole, sharing the same character, aims, and dispositions, working to the fulfilment of the same ends. In what manner are we to conceive of this union ?

It is facts of this kind which make Dualism an unsatisfactory philosophy. If Mind and Matter are simply different things, finding themselves together in the same world, but having no characteristics in common, it is hard to see how the one could be, or could even appear to be, produced by the other. It is hard to see how there can be so many intermediate steps between the entire mindlessness of a lump of lead and the full consciousness of a waking man. It is hard to understand the close mutual adaptation of each mind and the body which is its partner, the mind desiring just those things which are needed for the body's maintenance, and willing just those actions which the body is able to perform. If Dualism were the truth, we should be able to distinguish with complete sharpness between what is and what is not the work of the mind ; but we cannot do this—not even in the case of our own actions, where the conscious, sub-conscious, and unconscious seem inextricably commingled.

If Dualism is rejected, what alternatives remain ? I shall not put forward as the truth any one solution of our problem. Instead, I shall suggest three different lines of approach, any one of which, I think, may perhaps lead to the truth.

(A) The first alternative is to accept the main assumptions of Materialism as I have described it. The world is a unity ; there is only one kind of substance in it ; things differ from each other only in the manner of arrangement of their parts. There is then nothing in a living organism over and above the pieces of inorganic matter out of which it is compounded, and into which it will eventually be resolved. The differences in its behaviour, as compared with the inorganic, are only differences of complexity, resulting from more varied relations between its parts. Thus, in principle, everything can be accounted for by the laws of physics.

Now, to say that a state of consciousness *is* a re-arrangement of unconscious things or states seems to me to be complete nonsense. If, therefore, our theory is to be consistent, it must modify conventional notions of Matter to the extent of attributing some kind of consciousness, some kind of awareness, feeling, and striving, to the inorganic constituents of which a conscious organism is composed. Of course, it is not to be expected that one should clearly conceive what the consciousness of a lump of lead or of an atom is like. We may guess that it is more like our dream states than our waking states ; that it is much less varied in quality, the simpler things being aware of a much smaller range of features of their environment, and consequently capable of a much more limited range of actions in response to this awareness ; our variety of behaviour is a consequence of our variety of sensibility.

A theory of this kind gets a good deal of support from the scientific evidence, which reveals no break in the continuity of physical law between the inorganic and the organic. Its greatest drawback is that it is compelled to regard human consciousness as a composite thing, made up of many lesser consciousnesses. And this view is not easy to accept. For, it seems to me, though there is great complexity in what I am aware of, awareness itself is unitary ; it is the one " I " which knows. And though there is great complexity in my impulses and wishes, will is unitary ; it is the one " I " which decides. We cannot readily discover in consciousness any elements out of which it might be compounded ; nor can we find in it anything which can plausibly be regarded as constituting the consciousness of any particular physical part of the organism. There is nothing in the physical account of the situation to correspond to the unity of consciousness, or to explain how the elements of consciousness, whatever they may be, are held together in this peculiar unity.

(B) The second type of theory is one which holds that the mental is entirely derived from the non-mental, but also holds that mental phenomena are unique, and essentially distinct from any of the phenomena of inanimate Nature. Mind, it says, is wholly a product of the inanimate, but is nevertheless something quite different from the inanimate in character and mode of action, and not to be analysed away into something other than itself. This theory rejects the principle that there can be no more in the effect than in the cause, and allows the occurrence of absolute novelty in the universe ; the interaction of a number of things may produce something which is not like any of them or any combination of them. Life is a novelty produced by, or " emerging from," the lifeless ; and likewise mind is a novelty emerging from the mindless when it has reached a certain level of complication ; the unconscious adaptiveness of the lower organisms is succeeded by the deliberate purposiveness of the developed intellect. A human being is a physical object to which have been added the characteristics of life, and the further characteristics of mind. The mental is dependent on non-mental conditions for its coming into being ; but, having come into being, it operates according to its own nature. Thus we give up the materialist doctrine that the world is of one single stuff, to be explained according to one system of laws. We can allow the psychologist the free use of teleological explanations, of a type which would not be admissible in physics.

In other respects, however, this type of theory resembles Materialism. Mind is, in its view, a rarity in the universe, existing somewhat precariously on a non-mental foundation. Its appearance on the scene has been the fortuitous effect of purposeless material processes. There is no purpose or ' meaning " in the universe as a whole, except what we can succeed in putting there. The power of mind in the world is restricted to that which individuals, alone or in concert, can exercise over their own bodies, and through them on things in their neighbourhood. This is limited enough ; but at any rate the future is not inexorably fixed by physical facts ; there is always the chance that something greater than our minds may emerge from the cosmic process.

This is the kind of theory which is most economical in its assumptions, and ventures least far into the unknown. In consequence, it leaves a good deal to be accepted without explanation as brute fact. We must simply accept it as a fact that a congeries of unconscious physical processes can bring into existence a unitary conscious mind with properties quite unlike those of its producers. The only explanation we have any right to demand is a statement of the conditions under which this transformation occurs. Likewise, we must accept it as a fact that living things in whom mentality has not emerged are organised as though according to a plan, though there is in fact no plan and no planner. If we find these facts strange, we must just revise our standards of strangeness.

(C) The third alternative follows the Idealist tradition in supposing that Mind has not arisen out of not-Mind, but is a permanent and pervasive factor in the universe. Beside the examples of mentality observable here and there in men and animals, there is, let us suppose, a more comprehensive Mind which is their source, and which is also the cause of that purposive organisation of apparently mindless things.

Life on the earth shows some evidence of having sprung from a common source. But its history does not reveal to us the constant inexorable fulfilment of a single unchanging plan. It seems rather to be an experimental process in which different lines of development are tried in turn, not all of them successes. If there is one mind giving impetus and direction to the whole process of terrestrial life, it is a mind which changes, develops, and learns. Particular finite minds, we may suppose, branch off from the universal mind as the vehicles of particular projects ; it is in and through them that the cosmic purposes must be realised. The unity of consciousness is the unity of a pattern of living to be imposed upon a manifold of subsidiary activities.

As to inanimate nature, which is characterised by an unvarying, mechanical way of responding to stimuli, its function in a spiritual world may be compared to the function of habit in an individual personality. A reliable, automatic performance of subordinate bodily processes is necessary to give the soul adequate control over the body, and to allow the soul to concentrate its energies on thinking ahead and making new plans. Inanimate nature represents the fixed habits of the universal mind ; the initiation of novelty is confined to the souls of the living, just as in the individual organism control is concentrated in the brain. It is through the souls of living creatures, and on earth now principally through the souls of men, that cosmic development takes place.

That we are the vehicles of purposes broader and more far-reaching than our own may be made known to us in the sense of obligation, which draws us away from concern with our physical welfare and the assertion of our personalities, and interests us in the achievement of goods which we cannot ndividually enjoy. Conscience, indeed, is often flouted ; the world is an imperfect world, and the world-soul an imperfectly integrated soul. For spiritual progress is not just an advance from the worse to the better ; it is an advance from a narrower to a wider sphere of experience and action, in which, as we attain the opportunity of a richer and finer goodness, so we run the risk of a grosser and profounder evil. The Devil develops along with God.

In this progressive development, evolution is possible only because all living things die ; learning is possible because all habits may be outgrown. We cannot expect our own individual personalities to be more than temporary and provisional forms through which the universal mind expresses itself. But in being ourselves, we are not severed from the eternal source of all selves ; and in the profoundest experiences of religion we may know our ultimate oneness with God.

Such a theory as this is highly speculative. It goes far beyond the available evidence, and it is not easy to see what sort of scientific confirmation it could hope to secure. Matters might be different if, along these lines, one could produce an adequate explanation of " paranormal " psychical phenomena (telepathy, clairvoyance, precognition, etc.), with which materialist philosophy is so completely at a loss that a good many materialist thinkers have been driven to denying the established facts of the case ; but so far no explanation which looks at all adequate has been produced by anybody.

As it is, the grounds for preferring this type of philosophy to its alternatives are likely to lie less in theoretical considerations than in personal experiences, by which men have become convinced of the presence in the world of spiritual powers greater than themselves and their fellow-men. I do not think that such experiences can be conclusively shown either to be valid or to be invalid. If they are valid, I do not think we can claim that they give us a very full or precise knowledge of the purposes of God. The importance of a religious philosophy is not so much for our theories as for our

morale. If we do not properly understand the " meaning
life," at any rate we understand why men so persistentl
search for such a " meaning." The belief that we live in a
essentially spiritual universe may hearten us in the endeavou
to reach the best we can find in human life according to th
light that is in us.

FURTHER READING.

    For the general problem treated in this book :

    C. D. Broad—*The Mind and its Place in Nature.*
    C. F. Stout—*Mind and Matter.*
    C. Lloyd Morgan—*The Emergence of Novelty.*
    C. S. Sherrington—*Man on his Nature.*
    R. W. Sellars—*Evolutionary Naturalism.*
    F. H. Bradley—*Appearance and Reality.*
    G. Ryle—*The Concept of Mind.*

    For those who dislike long books :

    J. Wisdom—*Problems of Mind and Matter.*

INDEX